YOUNG WIDOWER

Young Widower

A Memoir

John W. Evans

University of Nebraska Press | Lincoln and London

18 FEB 2015

Mountain View, CA

Library of Congress
Cataloging-in-Publication Data
Evans, John W. (John William), 1977–
Young widower: a memoir /
John W. Evans. pages cm. — (River teeth
literary nonfiction prize)
ISBN 978-0-8032-4952-3 (pbk.: alk. paper)
ISBN 978-0-8032-5402-2 (epub)
ISBN 978-0-8032-5403-9 (mobi)
ISBN 978-0-8032-5401-5 (pdf) 1. Evans,
John W. (John William), 1977– 2. Evans,
John W. (John William), 1977– —Mar-
riage. 3. Widowers—United States—
Biography. 4. Young men—United
States—Biography. 5. Widowers—United
States—Psychology. 6. Widowhood—
United States—Case studies. 7. Wives—
Death—Psychological aspects—Case stud-
ies. 8. Loss (Psychology)—Case studies.
I. Title.
HQ1058.5.U5E93 2014
306.88'20973—dc23
2013032472

Set in Arno Pro by
Laura Wellington.
Designed by J. Vadnais.

This book is lovingly dedicated to Emma, Chloe, and Chase,
in Katie's memory.

While he was yet speaking, there came also another, and said, "Thy sons and thy daughters were eating and drinking wine in their eldest brother's house: And, behold, there came a great wind from the wilderness, and smote the four corners of the house, and it fell upon the young men, and they are dead; and I only am escaped alone to tell thee."
—Job, 1:18–19

Do we derive our comfort from the hope that you will hear us?
—Augustine, *Confessions*, 3.10

Contents

Acknowledgments

My thanks to Eavan Boland, Ken Fields, Justin St. Germain, Tarn Wilson, Ben Hubbard, Gail Drewes, Kelly Luce, Stephanie Wooley-Larrea, Thayer Lindner, Katherine Boyle, Michael Creeden, the Stanford Creative Writing Program, *River Teeth*, the University of Nebraska Press, and, above all, Cait.

Portions of this book have been published elsewhere, and I thank the editors for their care, especially Evelyn Somers at the *Missouri Review* and Isaac Fitzgerald at the *Rumpus*.

YOUNG WIDOWER

How Lives Go On

The year after my wife died, I compulsively watched television. I needed distraction, to be entertained. What I could not stream online or order through the mail I sought out at the local video store. I was living in a suburb of Indianapolis, about a mile from a strip mall where I could rent, in a pinch, midseason discs of *The Wire*, *The Office*, *Friday Night Lights*. I got to know the clerks by name, then their shifts, finally their tastes. Once, I tried to make a formal complaint against the corporate headquarters regarding the suspicious and perpetual absence of the fourth-season finale of *Battlestar Galactica*. It seemed unjust that the universe would conspire to deny my knowledge of its fictional origins. I worked up a good head of steam before leaving, distraught. I went back a few days later, during a different shift.

On my walks to the store, I listened to my wife's favorite songs. She was a huge country fan, especially mid-'90s radio country: Garth Brooks, the Judds, Randy Travis. As a child she had lived in rural, then exurban Illinois, attended college in central Minnesota. I didn't particularly like the music, but I enjoyed that it reminded me of her and also how the emotional range of the music never ran too far from the middle. The walks, however long, seemed to go more quickly.

My wife's death was violent and sensational. She was killed by a wild bear, while we were hiking in the Carpathian Mountains outside of Bucharest, where we had lived and worked for the last year of her life. She was thirty years old.

More than five hundred people attended the wake, held in her hometown. A cantor from the church led a John Denver sing-along, and several people spoke. A large dose of anxiety medication tempers what else I remember of that night. We formed a receiving line at the front door. We shook hands, hugged each other, looked down the line. Many of those arriving were strangers to me. As the night went on, my brother snuck me away to the basement, where someone from the funeral home had set out cookies and punch for the kids.

Numbness is a central feature of my first memories of that year. I learned to pantomime the real emotions I expected to feel, and that I believed were expected of me, until I felt safe with them. In this way I began to grieve. Every few weeks my doctor recommended a new activity: journaling, writing letters to my wife, going for walks in urban areas, getting a part-time job. In successively more direct ways, I engaged with the circumstances of my wife's death, then with my witnessing of it, and, finally, with her absence in the world.

At night, in my small room off the garage, I wrote out the sequence of my wife's death over and over. I sought an emotional directness more nuanced and honest than what I could manage in conversations with family and strangers. To anyone who might listen, I tried to express how and why I grieved. In my journal I tried to make sense of my own limitations as a husband and witness. As though I might take a kind of self-cure, I tried again and again to tell myself the end of a story interrupted by my wife's death.

I have three soft-cover notebooks in which I wrote daily accounts of my life during that year. The journal is a matter of will and record. I wanted to survive grief. I feared I would lose, with time, the intensity of my reactions. A therapist said we were personally and creatively redefining the context of my emotional experience of the world. I said it like this: What next? What now?

One of my part-time jobs was to tutor a high school student for his SAT exam. His parents were Nigerian. His mother, especially, had high expectations for his performance. Our relationship became cordial, then friendly. Finally, she asked me why I was living in Indiana. I knew how to answer the question in a vague but sufficient manner, enough to satisfy the social obligation while not sharing too much—*I am living with family while I sort out some job opportunities*—but with her I decided to speak frankly. Her response was complete, empathetic, and overwhelming. She said if I lived in Nigeria no one would mistake what I was enduring. In Nigeria there were complete rites of grief, ways of marking oneself to identify the loss; there were familial and social obligations and a period of time during which I would dress one way, speak another, eat a special diet, live in a specific manner and place. I explained that I was an American; our rituals and traditions of grief are private, self-sustained, piecemeal, and, ultimately, individual.

But that wasn't entirely right. If it was easy to substitute silence for strength, then it was also convenient to imply that certain uncomfortable facts should be declared or announced and so only said once. I should want my grief to end, as unmistakably as my wife's life had ended. To do so seemed polite, decent, and expected. How long would I live in Indiana?

My wife was born Kathryn Irene Garwood LaPlante. She was named for her maternal grandmother, Kathryn Garwood, and when we married, she took my last name. Kathryn Irene Evans. Katie.

I have in mind a memory from the last year of Katie's life. We are sitting on the balcony of our gray high-rise post-Communist-bloc apartment, overlooking one part of downtown Bucharest, drinking beer and eating cookies from a shop near her work. Katie is wearing fleece sweatpants and her brother Ed's red Indiana hoodie, circa 1986. The sweatshirt is frayed around the edges and collar. Her dark brown hair is pulled back. Her skin is bright and pale.

Katie has spent a Saturday morning at the office negotiating aid payments with the Romanian Orthodox Church. She is managing the country's first HIV/AIDS education program—I will say this with great pride when anyone asks—but the church insists on coupling the outreach with an existing domestic violence curriculum and so has doubled her workload while diminishing the impact of both projects. She is telling me about a colleague appointed to her office by the church, who treats the appointment like the sinecure it is. She looks tired.

That afternoon a long line of mourners leads a wooden casket on a horse-drawn cart through a park across the street. We take turns holding our digital camera out over the balcony, trying and failing to capture a close-up of this sprawling, seemingly endless procession. Is it a cultural celebration, a holiday? Is the dead person a dignitary, a celebrity? Are the processors family members? Designated mourners? We know nothing about the rite or its situation, but it is the first time we have seen such an event, so to us the occasion is significant, even romantic for its intrusion. Katie makes a note of it in her journal.

I can keep the memory of that afternoon fresh and at the front of my mind for a short while. I can run it backward and forward, focusing on one aspect, then another. I can take the scene wholesale and imagine watching it from the rooftop of the Athenaeum, on the other side of the park. The Athenaeum, with its domed mural of two thousand years of Roman, then Romanian, history, made into a single narrative. I can make an argument about Katie's work, the season, the city, our life together that year, that afternoon. Still, something distinct from my initial experience remains uncertain, however well I tell it. To whom am I telling these stories? What need do I have to make any argument?

On the day of her death, Katie will have read every poem I wrote during our time together. Many of those poems tell stories about us: as Peace Corps volunteers in Bangladesh, our families and friends, our work, teaching in Chicago, attending graduate school in Miami, moving for a year to Romania. Katie will have predicted which poems teachers and colleagues will like best. She will have suggested, time and again, that I speak more directly and clearly about experience and avoid petty ornamentation. We will have talked about her favorite poems—B. H. Fairchild's "The Blue Buick," Catherine Bowman's "Spice Night"—as models of the elegant and heartfelt writing we both admire.

A few months after the funeral, in the nature preserve where we scattered Katie's ashes, I read the parts of "The Blue Buick" that she admired most. "The Blue Buick" is a long narrative tribute to Fairchild's memory of a young couple whose arrival and stay transform his world and inspire his eventual departure for California. I turn off my phone and sit Indian-style on the ground, self-conscious. It is cold, sunny. The words are hard to distinguish in the glare. I mumble when strangers approach on the path:

She made a kind of smile that wavered at the end.
Life's been simplified for us. It's simple now.
But of course she was talking to herself, not me.
And I was thinking, this is it, how lives go on,
this is how it happens, what I do not understand.

I wonder whether this homemade rite honor Katie's absence or merely expresses my desire to understand it. I am trying not to articulate my grief in crude distinctions: then and now, here and there, she and I. The fact of Katie's death and her absence. Already Katie is becoming an object of grief, an occasion. I cannot avoid it. The Katie I address in the nature preserve will listen. She must. She is not there.

The morning after Katie died, my brother and sister flew from Chicago and New York to Bucharest. I met them at the airport and felt both ashamed and relieved to cry as they walked out from customs. That afternoon I tried to explain the shame and the relief to a psychiatrist at the embassy. How I had stayed up the whole night next to Katie's body, knowing she was dead, afraid to sleep. The doctor spoke in clear and simple phrases. We talked to each other in the broadest terms about death, bears, grief, mountains, travel, country music. I did not know this language yet. It was new, confusing, powerful. I tried to tell him a story about Katie, and as I spoke, I heard again her crying for help as she died, and I could not distinguish her voice from my own.

A week after the funeral, I moved to Indiana to live with Ed's family. I planned my day around their routines and gradually established my own. My two nieces left for their middle school at seven and returned at three. I got out of bed around eight. My nephew, the youngest, had just started kindergarten. Most mornings Ed's wife, Beth, walked their son to the bus stop. Some mornings, through the window, I would hear Ed starting his truck. He worked long hours as a contractor, and went rock-climbing every few weeks in Kentucky. Beth worked from home most mornings, but often we talked in the afternoons, ran errands together, and made lunch.

When it turned cold, I bought an electric blanket. My cats did not get along with the family pets, so I closed them into my room. All winter they sat under my desk lamp. In the spring they sat in the windowsill. Ed made bonfires in the side yard. That reminded me of mountains. On Katie's birthday we flew kites. At Christmas I drove to a friend's home in Vermont. One weekend I took a whiskey-tasting course at the local liquor store; Katie had liked Johnnie Walker, but I chose Glenmorangie. I took medications intermittently—orange sleeping pills, white anxiety pills. I developed a dry night cough, got strep, bronchitis. I convinced myself I was dying. I called the family doctor and demanded a TB screen. The test was negative. He suggested an allergy pill: I was allergic to my cats. He prescribed more sleeping pills.

Late mornings I heated oil in a pan until it smoked, poured in egg substitute to the rim, covered the top with cheese, flipped it, browned the cheese, and smothered the omelet with barbecue sauce. I ground four level tablespoons of Kenyan Special Blend and brewed coffee in a French press, then sat at the kitchen table and read the local paper. One day my name was mentioned in an editorial arguing for the construction of roundabouts to replace suburban traffic lights. I had talked to a woman outside the hardware store next to the franchise coffee shop at the strip mall, where I bought my groceries in the chain supermarket. I walked out from the cul-de-sac, down the street for six blocks, turned to another street, crossed the highway divider, and entered the parking lot. It took forty minutes to walk to the strip mall. It took seven minutes to make breakfast.

Some weekend evenings that first summer, I walked the kids across the state highway to the ice cream parlor. We counted cars, played games on the sidewalk, and waved at neighbors. We timed our crossing with stoplights at the exit ramps. At the height of rush hour cars would line up seven and eight deep. We ran to the divider, across traffic, and up the embankment. I carried my nephew on my shoulders, so that he could keep pace. We arrived as-the-crow-flies to our destination and chose among forty-odd flavors, then stood at the bright pink-and-blue plastic counters, with double and triple scoops. We walked out into the heat, back across the highway.

On a blog about Katie I tried to say simple, direct things about grief, loss, and absence. I annotated photographs for friends and family. I responded to comments. I posted links to Katie's favorite songs, movies, and books and asked anyone who might synchronize witness and understanding to fill in the gaps. If there was no consistent perspective from which to render the memory of Katie's death or to remember the feeling in our marriage, then I could at least wonder earnestly about this quiet and understated observer who hoped he might one day become the ringleader, the unifying presence around which everyone now gathered to remember and grieve for Katie.

Wasn't Katie still my wife more than someone else's high school friend or college roommate?

A life that Katie and I had started six years earlier was the beginning of the life I lived now in Indiana. I said it over and over in therapy, but I wasn't sure there was a continuity at all. In-laws were no longer in-laws. Minor anecdotes anticipated a different life. A home in a city where I had never before lived contained photographs of a childhood Katie, whose ashes were clumped in the soil of her hometown in a different state. I would never again visit the country where she had died. I could make no permanent life anywhere. I wanted no life after our life.

Don't put the horse before the cart, the therapist said. *Take it in small pieces, one at a time.*

Much of Katie's life went missing from what I wrote on the blog and said to other people. Friends, family histories, secrets, fights: I did not actively exclude them, but I did not invite them into conversations, either. A polite consensus simplified certain silences. I told myself that what I omitted protected a fragile recovery; that I was not exploiting Katie's death, but rather being noble in the face of adversity; that I was distinguishing the occasion of my sorrow from its origin. The silences, I believed, somehow protected other people from *what they should never have to know*. But that was nonsense. To begin the story in Indiana rather than Romania meant I wasn't just putting the cart before the horse; I was insisting that, really, I had been pushing the cart all along.

We had gone with our friend Sara to Busteni, a few hours north of Bucharest, to celebrate my thirtieth birthday. Our guidebook said there were hostels on the ridge with rooms to let. At the trailhead we met a Romanian on holiday and two Israelis celebrating their honeymoon. We hiked together all day in clear weather: trails, waterfalls, rockslides, switchbacks, lakes. We arrived at the first hostel about an hour before sunset. There were no vacancies, but the kitchen was still open. We ate a dinner of pork soup, pickled vegetables, stale bread, and cold beer. Katie and I took a picture by a kilometer marker showing the highest point of the peak. Then we set out in two groups—me and the Israelis at the front; Katie, Sara, and the Romanian following—to walk the mile or so to the next hostel.

Just after dusk, at a long turn in the path, we noticed that Katie's group had fallen behind. The Israelis went ahead, while I waited at a stream. Glacial ice was melting on the ridge, and there was enough water to make crossing in the dark tricky. When Katie's group didn't come, I hiked back up the trail to find them. It was darker now. I followed one trail, but it led in the wrong direction. I doubled back toward the first hostel, whose light I could see in the distance. Near the kilometer marker, I found pages from our guidebook strewn on the ground, next to Katie's backpack and shoes. I yelled her name. I tried to walk in circles, remembering an old Boy Scout trick about not getting lost. From about twenty yards off the trail Katie called back. *Don't come closer. Find a gun. Get back quickly.*

The trail was rocky and hard to follow at night. I kept losing my footing. I fell. I got up. The second hostel also had a porch light. A group of tourists standing under it were waving at me. The Romanian, they explained, had escaped the bear and run ahead of me to the hostel. Now they were watching for other survivors. Sara was running down the trail, too. She was just behind me. Katie was alone on the ridge.

Inside the hostel the owner refused to give me his rifle. With so many witnesses, he kept insisting, he would be fined for discharging a gun without a state permit. His business would be ruined. I tried to buy the rifle with American dollars. I offered to trade my passport for it. Instead he called for a hunting patrol from a nearby village.

I stumbled back to the trail. Three men staying at the hostel followed at a distance. It was hard to find the kilometer marker again. When we saw the bear and heard Katie's cries, the three men ran. I stood now ten, maybe fifteen yards from Katie, shining my flashlight across the ridge. I had a better view of the bear: large, brown, straddled over Katie, dipping its head back and forth across her torso, with white fur on its front paws and muzzle.

I sat up all night with Katie's body. Three doctors from nearby cities arrived to certify her death. They defaced Katie's body with various crude tests—eyelid check, stethoscope, CPR, reflexes— that only confirmed the obvious. I remember that as each took turns compressing her chest, I could hear ribs crack. I wondered how the eventual autopsy would distinguish this trauma from the bear attack. Probably, it wouldn't.

I understood immediately that there would be a funeral, an obit-
uary, explanations, maybe at some point accusations, clarifications,
and misunderstandings. I don't know why I was thinking about it.
I imagined it: standing in the first few pews of the church in Illinois
with the faux-gothic exterior and uncomfortable wood benches.
The spread of food in the basement after the service. In a diner
across the street, people who grieved for Katie might ask questions,
then decide to blame me, hate me, or feel genuinely sorry for me.
I was a witness now and a young widower. I did not know any witnesses of bear attacks or young widowers. Someone thought to
cover Katie's body, and as the night went on, I started to fear it.
Whose body was under the tarp? Katie's body was under the tarp.

In Indiana my taste in television evolved. I became suspicious of
representations of suffering, especially gratuitous violence. What
was the point of imagining bloodlust and apocalypse, if not to enjoy
it? I preferred alternative logics—superheroes, universes, Texas—
and comedies. They rejected finality. I found comfort in their rep-
etitions. What did it matter that I was real and the people I watched
were not? I felt present by proxy in constant variations on redemption: charity, sublimation, self-actualization. Even the most icono-
clastic and antinarrative shows—*Seinfeld*, *The Larry Sanders Show*,
Lost, *The Sopranos*—eventually grounded relationships in longev-
ity, delivered moral comeuppances, and established continuities
where none seemed to exist. Successful series—*X-Files*, *Battlestar
Galactica*—generated spinoffs. Writers pursued in new series the
subject matter, stylistic flourishes, and ideas that had interested
them in previous ones. A habit of continuation had the ironic effect
of making it *feel* like my favorite shows never really went off the air,
when in fact it was the stories themselves that repeated and there-
fore resisted closure.

Sometimes, after I returned a disc or checked out a new one, I
stopped in at the chain bookstore across the street. I poked through

tall displays of bestsellers and new releases, then the poetry and magazine racks, and finally, inevitably, the self-help aisle. It seemed to be the largest section in the store. *Personal Growth—Grief* targeted a demographic three, four, and five decades older than my own. Wistful elders looked out plaintively from dust jackets; they seemed to reach out to each other, around me, across titles and spines. Sometimes just a hand filled the cover, or a nature scene, a gravesite, a blank white page marked with the singular, patronizing jargon of consolation. *Coping. Grieving. Making Sense.* I tried to imagine the subsection where I would find some particular instruction after Katie's death:

Personal Growth—Grief—Animal Attack—Bear—Coward
Personal Growth—Grief—Young Widower—Survivor—Hopelessness
Personal Growth—Grief—Youth—Widowed—Blank Slate—Free
Personal Growth—Grief—Violence—Witness—Failed Husband

I bought books and did my best to read them. It was reassuring, even comforting, to see their titles stacked neatly on my bedside table each night. I might glean, without intention, some cumulative wisdom. With enough time I could pursue recovery. For now my room was filled with dubious comforts: sleeping pills, anxiety pills, allergy pills, earplugs, antacids, a humidifier, a white noise machine.

Ed, ten years Katie's senior, was nearly her physical twin: slender framed, square jawed, dark features and those same light blue eyes. Friends and neighbors remarked on the resemblance constantly, though at first I didn't see it. Ed didn't *really* look like Katie to me, but he told many of the same family stories. He smiled, paused extra beats for jokes, and shuffled across rooms with Katie's easy grace. Sometimes, when he did not act like Katie—his voice inflecting in slow turns between words, his sense of humor less sharp—I was surprised to feel disappointment at the divergence.

Those first weeks in Indiana, Ed and I went everywhere together, out for walks, to movies, to the city park near his house. We drove his truck to new neighborhoods to do advance work for his tuck-pointing business. Everywhere, chimneys stood in disrepair, magnificent houses with satellite dishes and two or three exposed joints worn through. The recession was a boom time for home repairs: people did what they could to stem the loss of their home's value. On the roofs, Ed explained, he could get a better sense of the damage. We wrote down addresses, so that Ed could return the next morning, or week, to pitch an estimate.

At night we sat on the back porch smoking clove cigarettes, Katie's favorite. The sugared filter was sweet on my lips, the nicotine strong and heavy in my lungs. My head seemed to lift a little from my shoulders, and it felt good to say everything I could think to say, to talk about Katie and not hold anything back. I saw no reason to know things about Katie and not share them with the people who had loved her.

The late-summer Indiana heat relented a little earlier each night. In the dark I could see less and less of Ed, but I heard his voice. Really, we both knew something about Katie that the other person did not. We traded these stories like two kinds of currency: Katie's childhood for her adult life and ambitions. The gap between us was something to narrow. Already close, we made a new bond of getting to know Katie better through each other's eyes: the little sister with whom Ed grew up and the wife who had been my best friend.

There was another side to this proximity. Each time we talked, I stemmed the low level, persistent guilt for how much I still loved Katie's family and for how my enjoyment of that connection seemed only to intensify in the days and weeks after her death. We grieved together. We grew closer. If the guilt was tangible, real, and unavoidable, then so too was the affection. I worried what would happen if I ever became, in their eyes, unsympathetic.

I had wanted to survive Katie's death in Romania; now, in Indiana, something beyond grief insisted still on survival, as though I were courting some second life, free of the obligations and structures of the first. It might never be so certain and stable, or insulated and naïve, but it would be entirely my own. Anything might happen next. I was grieving but healthy. I had been married before and liked it. A certain undeniable hopefulness twinned with the sense of debt, proportionally, as though each should only magnify the other.

Perhaps Katie's death protected me now and made me a kind of talisman to the people I loved. The sheer improbability of the circumstances of her death could make all of us exempt, I thought, by association, from such future calamity. More and more, it seemed, I could hardly remember that night myself. I had gone up one side of the mountain with Katie. I had come down the other side with her body.

After fights, or to get a rise out of me, Katie was fond of singing the chorus to Joni Mitchell's "The Circle Game." I understood that she meant to explain something about her feelings and also to draw a contrast between the trauma in her life and the absence of trauma in my own. In high school she had rolled a conversion van on a rural highway and walked away with minor injuries. After her parents divorced, she had lived with her grandfather during the end of his life. One brother had died suddenly, while we were in the Peace Corps, from complications following a common illness. Katie's sister had lost a daughter in childbirth. Loss was, if not an entirely common experience, then something to anticipate and expect. Katie found little to admire in its denial.

On my desk in Indiana, I arranged a few objects. A roll of candies that Katie liked. A framed photo of us on the ridge. Her St. Christopher medal. At the strip mall one day I purchased a large pumpkin-spice candle. The next time I sat down to write, I arranged the objects into a new order. I lit the candle and moved our photo off to the side. I didn't like that emphasis. So I switched them. I taped loose photographs on the wall. The metal on a tulip engraving that Katie had given me for a birthday present began to peel. I stacked some pocket texts on top of it. I took rocks from the garden to prop everything in place. Before her last trip to the Republic of Georgia, Katie had left a miniature plush Paddington on my pillow. I turned him so that the tag (*Please look after this bear*) faced toward me. Over time I added to the arrangement. I took to tending it a little each time I sat down to write. A map of Bucharest. Some letters and a bandanna. Individually they were bric-a-brac and hodge-podge. Together they were a place made sacred by association. A shrine.

Katie is not the intellectual experience of a grieving mind. I wrote this over and over in my journal, but it was not quite right.

I had no shrine in my home until I built one. For a while I added to it.

I will not rebuild the shrine. It was a temporary and important place for acknowledgment. I have other places now more permanently sacred to me: Indiana, Katie's hometown, the nature preserve where we spread her ashes. One I can begin to approach now, if only on the page and in memory: a mountain ridge in Eastern Europe. I hope to never visit it again. I wrote most mornings in Indiana my confusion, then my guilt, Katie's work and life, the story of our marriage, and finally my memory of that day. The shrine grew with what I added to it. And it is lost forever.

There Are No Words

At the end of a long workday, Katie walks barefoot the mile or so from our apartment building near Revolution Square to the bar-basement Teatrul Act in Bucharest's city center. Though I am not there to see it, a friend says years later in a letter that Katie is smiling: looking for me. *As though,* the friend writes, *she was on an adventure.*

In fact, Katie has locked herself out of our apartment, while chasing the cat. And because I do not write down how she told it to me later that night, I can only imagine she must have paused a moment outside our door, then thought it was a beautiful spring day to walk anywhere; to stretch her legs a bit even on the hot pavement and busy streets would be a nice change of pace. She arrives at the theater, watches me rehearse my lines, and perhaps even laughs a little, proud; Katie likes watching me when I don't know she's there. In a play about America I am a cartoon tyrant, a corrupt state governor manufacturing a mild virus for profit. The English-language comedy runs three nights. *Epidemic of Fear: The Influenzical!*

Always, whenever Katie walks into a room, I think I can't miss it—a Christmas tree on fire, a loyal and friendly dog—but that afternoon, even in my imagination, she is gone before I see her, finding our keys in my bag and leaving a note I do not keep. We will see each other later. She pauses a moment to make small talk with the friend whose letter becomes my only occasion to make this witness. In that last year of her life, on everyone she meets, Katie makes such an impression. The memorial service in the basilica is packed with friends, students, colleagues, and strangers.

It's not just that Katie was strong and lovely, the friend writes, *not just her dark hair and blue eyes, her charming and easygoing nature; all of her was just so beautiful.*

Even in memory—in my imagination—can't I stop the moment long enough to turn and watch her leave? Didn't I always admire the sadness of her absence and the occasion of my temporary solitude? Over and over I turn it in my mind. My beautiful wife. My Katie. What the poet calls the elusive particular against *the luminous clarity of a general idea.* Katie walking across the city to find me, without her shoes. How I could be useful and loved by her in that moment. However minor, that part of her life continued without my help.

Six months after we leave the Peace Corps and move to Chicago, Katie and I drive north and west from the city to the Theater at Marriot Resort Hotels in Lincolnshire, Illinois, to spend the weekend with her family.

I am wearing a light blue oxford shirt with gray wool slacks, thin dress socks, and freshly polished penny loafers. The shirt and pants have been tailored by a man named Iqval, in his small shop in the city in Bangladesh where I have worked and lived for the previous two years. Katie knows the shop. She likes Iqval. Whenever she visited my town, we would sometimes stop there on the way from the bus stand, to buy him tea and talk about his favorite American sport, professional wrestling.

That first winter back in the United States, Katie and I get in the habit of running three or four miles most nights along the paths that face Lake Michigan. Katie is a natural athlete. I notice it especially when we run, her long and easy jogging stride, her slender runner's ankles. She almost always legs out the last stretch at a faster pace. I can't help admiring from a distance Katie's slight shoulders, her high cheekbones, and the pale blue eyes that, watering against the cold, flush with our semirace, her clear victory, looking back at me. Waiting. In such moments Katie exudes vulnerable and immodest strength, well in excess of her cautious talent for being naturally good at many things; the mix of strength and humility that ironically makes her, for so many people, essentially, undeniably "Katie."

Sometimes, Katie shuffles to a stop during our runs. Her ankle, which has never quite healed after a fantastic sprain, swells and clicks at the slightest instability. She has yet to see the doctor who will diagnose a permanent structural flaw in the ankle, one that requires periodic anti-inflammatories and rotating braces to keep the joint from moving too far outside its natural range of motion. With time these interventions only mitigate the severity of the injuries that come, on hikes and runs, even long walks, more and more frequently.

We arrive at the Lincolnshire a few hours ahead of the rest of her family. I am all dressed up for no good reason. I remember worrying that the mud on the shoe leather might ruin its finish, that I shouldn't sit too long if I want everything to look freshly pressed. I stand in the pool deck, bouncing on the balls of my feet. Eventually, we check into our room and unpack our bags. We put on our running clothes and set out into the late-winter cold to find the jogging tracks that circle the resort.

After our first lap Katie stops, covers her eyes, smiles, and waves to the parking lot. Ed, Beth, and their two young daughters are unloading the family van after a long drive from Indianapolis. For all of the adoring stories Katie tells, alternating wonder and frustration, Ed is much smaller than I expect, five-feet-seven maybe. He takes his time saying hello, pretending to look me over, reaching high over my head to confirm that, indeed, I am six feet and seven inches tall, as Katie has told him. Beth, his wife, smiles and gives me a quick hug; she is eight months pregnant with their first boy. The girls hold back, standing with their mother, shy and polite. I carry their bags to their rooms. A few hours later Katie's mother, Judy, calls from the lobby to say she and her husband have arrived with Katie's sister and niece. We should all meet in the lobby and check out the pool.

I have met Judy once before, over dinner, the week before Christmas. It was a formal occasion at the nicest restaurant in Katie's hometown, with heavy tablecloths, dim lighting, a full bar, and very good manners. At that dinner Judy's husband discussed new fronts in the War on Christmas; I tried to make small talk, asking questions about a family I knew only in the broadest details, from stories Katie told me on another continent. Even then Katie's family seemed so large—six or seven aunts, a few dozen cousins—that I got to worrying I would screw up someone's name, mistaking a brother for an uncle or a great-aunt for a niece. Judy was kind and generous, a little distracted; holding back, maybe, curious to see if things might really take between Katie and me now that we were back in the United States.

At the resort I see Judy in what I later know to be her truest and happiest element: relaxed and vibrant, surrounded by the adult children who adore her, a little nervous for the weekend's plan, but hopeful and optimistic. I see her smiling the same bright-eyed smile Katie sometimes unwittingly breaks out, the one that, when she knows someone is watching her, quickly settles into a more modest grin.

That weekend I do not get my chance to wear what Ed will later, and regularly at family events, call my "church clothes." I do spend hours in the pool, tossing one child after another high and into the deep end. I sit at dinner, making still more small talk, then dancing in the resort lounge with Judy and the nieces. Both nights, we play 4-5-6 dice with Katie's cousins for three dollars a hand. I sneak off with Ed to the gaming room, a small converted closet that just fits a Galaga–Ms. Pac-Man stand-up console, a quarters machine, and a broken foosball table. We take turns playing both games late into the night, buying each other beers.

I take to Ed right away. He is kind, a little mannered, but a genuine and decent guy. I really like Beth, who seems to read and listen to everything. I think we will manage an easy alliance of outsiders to the family.

Our last night at the resort, Ed and I sit at the bar watching the end of a basketball game and talking about high school. When Katie joined the cross-country team, Ed explains, the coach gave her a teddy bear, saying she would need it because, following Ed, she had awfully big shoes to fill. Katie has told me this story before, but as Ed and I sit there drinking now, I come to understand a part of it differently. Ed is proud of his little sister for following in his footsteps, but he is also worried she might feel stuck in his shadow. He believes it is a given that she can, and will, with time come into her own, but he's not sure she wants to do it. In his mind the placard on the gymnasium wall containing their names is a marker for her beginning, rather than his end.

And so, Ed explains, it was a shock when Katie quit the team her senior year, gave up competitive running altogether, and focused instead on graduating from high school a semester early. He does not know what to make of the full scholarship to the small state college in rural Minnesota that followed that spring, or the move that summer, or especially, four years later, her decision to leave Minnesota altogether and join the Peace Corps in Bangladesh. What does Katie hope to get away from, Ed asks, and how far does she have to go to do it? Is she coming back home, now, for good?

I say that I have not thought much about these questions. Really, they are Katie's to answer.

In Bangladesh, I tell Ed, Katie seemed so eager to move back to Chicago, to be near her family. Now that we are living in Chicago, and she is settled into a daily life, she seems restless with the long-term picture. What we are doing together, the plans we want to make eventually, the jobs we think we might want for ourselves: all of these are conversations that begin and end in the broadest terms, sometimes with a fight, often after only a few sentences.

I tell Ed that Katie is beautiful, strong, and happy. But she does not like expectations. She will not prove anything to anyone. She thrives in the moment, in a way that I find both attractive and unsettling. How can anyone seem so able to walk away from anyone and anything? How has she, in fact, done exactly that so many times before, in anecdotes and conversations about her family and life? The year, according to Katie, or the years, according to Ed, she and he just didn't speak? Will she and I one day follow the same pattern? If so, why is she choosing me now?

The next morning I feel stupid for confiding so much in Ed. Surely, I tell myself, I had too much to drink and let down my guard.

But there is another part to my indiscretion; one that, however unaware I am of it in the moment, lays the groundwork for a closeness I cherish immensely during Katie's life. It takes form, not in wholesale drunken declarations, but in the careful and quiet practices of disclosure, the sense of exception to her life that being loved by Katie allows me.

At last call I tell Ed that, secretly, I have always wanted people to call me "Jack." Jack Kennedy, London, Gilbert, Kerouac, Nicholson, even C. S. "Jack" Lewis. I like the idea of being the sort of person everyone knows formally by one name and informally by another. I tell Ed that I have always secretly wanted to be anyone else; that this other person I mean to become requires those qualities natural to Katie, which I have never mastered: discretion, distance. The sense, always, that one carries internally a secret born of a different life.

Ed tries "Jack" out that night, and for the next couple of years he takes every occasion to address me by it, alternately teasing and reminding me of my request, until finally, one afternoon years later, I ask him, please, to just call me "John." I say at the time that my opposition is instinctual—I just can't get used to hearing the new name—but I also feel dishonest for the easy rationalization. Ed is teasing me. I don't like being teased. If it is stupid to think now, after Katie's death, that the point of a name could only be the truth it accumulates in repetition and practice, then at the time I feel deeply relieved to be free of a childish fantasy. I am irrevocable in my own way; I am also, perhaps, too easily influenced.

As we leave the resort that weekend, Katie says it is the first time since her brother Richard's death a little more than a year before that her whole family, except for their father, has gathered together in the same place. She has been thinking of Richard all weekend, just as she is sure Judy, Ed, and her sister have kept his memory close. If I had known the death date, or thought to ask Katie then to name the absence or even to ask later why she held it back, then I understand during our drive that we are very much still at the beginning of our relationship. Some part of the gap between us remains unmeasured. I can only know, as she tells it to me one afternoon in Bangladesh, the fact of Richard's death. I cannot yet recognize his absence in Katie's life.

In the car that afternoon, I do not want to push too hard to know more about Richard. Here is the first and most essential tension in my life and marriage with Katie; she needs secrets, and she needs me to trust that those secrets, even when she eventually discloses them, are kept for good reasons. I cannot distrust her for them. I cannot resent her for needing them. And, however wrong it feels to be either excluded or indignant because of what she is not ready to tell me, I must not push her. She does not want comfort. Perhaps she believes I will one day understand her grief or, worse, misunderstand it.

Where our marriage seems now to close back upon itself, between the two places of Richard's death (beginning) and Katie's death (end), I try to make my year in Indiana the hinge. That first week a poet friend writes by email to say, *There are no words for your loss, John,* and I think, *Isn't that your duty? Shouldn't poets spend all day finding words to make loss real to strangers?* The anger is generative. I write my first poem for Katie a few days later and publish it on my blog. I call it "There Are No Words." I write in my journal, *There must be words for absence too finite for loss.* Then, as now, I think I understand something about how easily after one unimaginable loss another can follow. In this way, thinking of Richard, I feel closer to Katie. For a time after her death, I am very eager to hear stories about Katie's life, especially stories about us. I think they might refresh some certainty of feeling I have yet to understand as stable, neutral memory: a glimpse of the real thing alternately revealed in parts of a whole, held back and kept together.

From Teatrul Act, I walk home and sit with Katie on our balcony, watching a funeral procession and drinking cold beer. From the Lincolnshire Theater, Katie and I drive home to Chicago, where our new life together continues to begin, a life I hope will become a marriage, which continues now as the story of Katie's life and the fact of my grief after it. I stand in either place from time to time, willing her story to become either elegy or narrative. The consequence of not keeping that impossible middle means some last part of Katie cannot close down into feeling and anecdote. It is the remainder of a grief that infinitely carries forward. It must be expressed.

Losing the Marriage

After Katie's death, I kept two rings in a box. The first was white gold with a polished blue opal. The second was rose gold with an oval-cut ruby. I purchased the opal ring in Chicago for the anniversary of our first date and the ruby ring a year later in Chennai, during a six-week teacher's trip to India. Both were supposed to be engagement rings. Four, maybe five times, I meant to ask Katie to marry me, then lost my nerve. Katie was ambivalent about marriage. I was eager to marry and terrified she might say no. We fought about what her reluctance meant for our relationship and future. Better, I told myself, to wait and try later.

Those first months after her death I wanted some of what belonged to Katie to remain my own. I wanted to keep whole and vital certain parts of her life that were already losing shape.

It was a waning effort. Memory and grief, I quickly understood, made no meaningful complement. Each time I took down the box from the shelf, I felt as though I was begging some last bit of juju. *Startle the sound of her laugh. Bring back her smile all at once.* Where was the general shock of grief, the certainty of missing the Katie I knew for seven years? I wanted to lie in bed all day and wallow; to wail and moan; to collapse, withdraw, and never recover.

I couldn't do it. At the time I thought it meant the worst about my character and our marriage. I was insufficient to grief. I was a coward who would not face my feelings directly. I had never really loved Katie, and only a few weeks after her death I could hardly recall us. I preferred instead to dwell on the end of her life. Only much later did it occur to me that this should be what happens at the end of a marriage: I am able to lose it.

I say "losing the marriage" because I can no longer describe how I loved that life. It is no longer present for me.

This is part of what grief does to memory. The feelings are intercut with long gaps—the sound of a voice, the lost afternoon—that widen like dark spaces on film run too many times through the projector. The obligations are certain and particular—places, dates, words—but around them is only the suggestion of feeling: the image, bright light shining through it, a room refusing to stay dark.

I didn't mean to lose the marriage, that center of a life we alternately celebrated and endured and for which we both made compromises, locating in a certain honesty the truth of why and how we loved each other; that it was a marriage, hard-fought and won.

I imagined that after, or maybe because of, Katie's death the marriage would be magnified; a dignified widowhood would bring forward its best parts in a kind of nostalgic wash. I fantasized about holding court with friends and family members, sharing colorful anecdotes about our honeymoon and intercontinental adventures, avuncular, sympathetic, entirely separate of Katie's death and absence and the continuing life after it.

When Katie died, I was twenty-nine years old. She was thirty. Every two years we moved to a new place: Bangladesh, Chicago, Miami, Romania. We were volunteers in the Peace Corps, teachers in high schools, working professionals, and graduate students. Always, we tried to keep some option for the future unsettled, so that we might see ourselves as individuals joined in a common life.

A week before her death, Katie applied for a public health job in Malawi. I read about the country's per capita income (low), foreign debt obligations (high), highlands (vast), infant mortality (egregious). Was Malawi a home I would come to like more than Romania or Bangladesh? Was it the place, unlike Chicago or Miami, where a more permanent-seeming life might finally begin? Could we have started a family there? Before Katie's death, it did not seem important to make these kinds of choices. We either did not want the obligations, or we didn't know we wanted them. Wherever we went next, I thought, someone will need a public health official, and someone else will want an affable English teacher. I will teach my classes. At the end of the school day I will cross whichever city to Katie's office and wait while she finishes her work and shuts down her computer. Then we will head out together to dinner, for drinks, to the shops, to a friend's house or the countryside for the weekend, maybe to the cinema to watch the latest American movie. And when her contract is finished, we will start to feel restless. We will consider our options, make a decision, and see what comes along next.

The medieval walled city, birthplace of Vlad the Impaler, was guarded that year, as it had been for centuries, by bell ringers greeting tourists in forty languages. Good friends, Dave and Meghan, visited from Chicago for the week, on their way to Hungary. We had planned the trip with them as much to watch the scenery as to see the place. It was spring. Snow still peaked the taller mountains off the track. We wore heavy jackets and drank long espressos as we rode the train through tunnels and valleys. We moved to the forward compartment of the new express rail—lightweight, sleek—and for the first half of the journey, we were the only passengers.

Dave and I sat together by the window, talking about Chicago. Much, he explained, had changed since Katie and I left our apartment in Uptown three years earlier. Our favorite bowling alley had closed suddenly that New Year's Eve, sold to developers; a parking garage was already up in its place. Ross and Melissa were gone to Wisconsin for graduate school and engaged. Sarah and Jason lived now in Seattle. They had a son. Everyone else, it seemed, was headed for the near-north suburbs, commuting still to the city, but starting families.

Dave was handsome and modest, an exceptional bowler. He had the habit of genuinely apologizing when he won, as though he enjoyed the victory but hated beating me. He had recently been promoted, so he could finally start to pay down his student-loan debt and save for retirement, family, a house. They had purchased life, term, and disability insurance. They had written wills and advance directives, given powers of attorney, and named beneficiaries and legal guardians. Meghan would quit working, if she wanted to; they were thinking hard about having a baby sooner rather than later. Dave wanted a big family, like the one he had married into, but Meghan was less certain about a number. Mostly, he said, it would be a matter of timing. The clock was ticking.

Children and parenting was a conversation Katie and I could never quite begin. We doted on nieces and nephews. We were good with babies. We had always imagined ourselves individually as adults with children. Together, we were less certain. How would parenting alter a life that valued speed, work, and travel? Would our children inherit, from either side of the family, certain illnesses and conditions? The prospect of caring long term for a sick or disabled child terrified Katie. She dreamed about it frequently.

Other considerations were less hypothetical. We had decided to marry as much to stay together as to continue a life we both liked. Would we really stay together long enough to raise a child? Did we want our longer life to follow those patterns that had established the shorter one? A lot of people seemed to be doing this, though now many of them were having babies. Wasn't it so very ordinary to think about settling somewhere where we might want to work, live, *and* raise a family?

I was happy for Dave. I liked that he was so pleased. As I listened and took mental notes to fill in the details later with Katie, I wondered how she was managing what must have been a similar conversation with Meghan. Katie had noticed that trip how Dave and Meghan kept referring to themselves as "a family." Their ambitions, like their marriage, were the beginning of something to which they were committed, rather than its continuation or end. I envied their certainty. Here was a corollary that said marriages worked with planning and thrived on certainty with the best of intentions. Like bowling with Dave, however competitive I felt, I couldn't help rooting for the guy.

Katie was skeptical of the convention. Weren't there other reasons to make a life together, and did the comparison between motives have to seem so stark? You need kids to have a family, Katie and I agreed later that night, and it didn't feel so defensive as it does now. We took comfort in a certain resignation. Perhaps we worried: could that ever be us?

That first year in Chicago, when Katie wore the opal ring I gave her as a birthday present, I sometimes imagined it meant we *were* engaged. I enjoyed the fantasy. I told my brother, over nachos, that I planned to propose. And yet, when it came time to pop the question, the precious events I had so clearly imagined lost their sequence. I did not drop to one knee at our favorite restaurant, announce my intentions, and bravely smile. I knew Katie might say no, and I didn't want my fantasy to end in rejection. So, instead, I hedged. I made more reservations. We walked out to Lake Michigan, along the path, and talked about how much we liked each other. I fumbled at the ring box in my pocket. I told her to open it, and when she looked up at me, uncertain, I said that by no means was I proposing marriage, but wasn't it a fantastic ring?

Each time I failed to propose, our life continued. Katie liked the opal ring: its elegance and simplicity. And I liked very much that she liked it.

At the school where I taught seventh-grade social studies, we waited daily for the results of the annual state exam. Would we be judged competent teachers or poor ones? Were our students exceedingly capable or merely below average? To pass the time, the science teacher and I put together a play for the spring assembly. The students lined up in neat rows under American flags, then ran full-tilt toward the stage, screaming, while I played the guitar. It was the Battle of Bull Run. Over and over we practiced it on the playground. Stand stock-still, sprint, stop on a dime. Again, and this time really stick your spot. In her introduction the principal celebrated our idealism and national spirit. Most parents worked, though the few that attended cheered politely. Three weeks from the end of our school year, I thought, *Have we come to the end of another year already?*

I took the bus east to the lake, then south to Katie's apartment. We had eaten lobster bisque a few weeks earlier in Lincoln Square.

Now, I wanted to surprise Katie by making the same dinner at home. I stopped at the grocer behind Katie's building for butter, cream, sherry and brandy, clam juice. I dug into the back of the deep freezer and found six gray lobster shells wrapped on blue Styrofoam board in tight plastic, one-quarter pound each, three for ten dollars. I bought two bottles of wine and a loaf of fresh bread.

The windows in Katie's studio fogged a little as I worked. The key, I thought, was to keep everything moving in a smooth procession. I found a small blue wire colander, which I balanced in the sink. I had boiled the shells for two hours, and now I needed to separate the stock from the boiled meat. The edges of the pot were hot as I lifted it from the burner. I turned to the sink and slowly, carefully poured the contents of the pot through the fine middle mesh. The lobster was translucent and fell off the shell into a neat pile. The stock poured into the drain. I had forgotten to put a pot under the colander. Even as I realized my mistake, I admired the sheen the liquid made on the steel as it bubbled and disappeared.

I panicked. I refilled the pot. Perhaps some of the reserve fluid gummed onto the metal would come out with a second boil. The shells themselves were clean and shiny, steaming a bit. I dropped them back into the pot and scraped the meat stuck in the colander. I boiled the shells for half an hour, then did my best to follow the rest of the recipe.

Now Katie's small room reeked of fish and onion. Froth blackened under the coil. How had I managed to make such a mess? As a last resort I poured the watery mess into two bowls, dropped into each a tablespoon of heavy cream, and sprinkled a garnish of fresh tarragon. I pressed toast to the bottom of the bowls, so that the cream and tarragon seemed to float at the surface of a rich broth. I sat down on the floor, cross-legged, and pulled over the futon—it was our bed, our sofa, our makeshift dining table—and lit candles, listening for the elevator. I paused Katie's favorite song at the chorus, so that it might begin with her first steps through the door.

Say it wasn't the perfect marriage. When we were happy, we made choices, rather than decisions. When we fought, the distinctions became explicit and difficult. I don't know whether this makes our life together easier or harder, less or more conventional, and none of this really is practical now; I am attracted only to the speculation, a grayness that yields neither color nor its absence. We looked at every option before us and followed out gut. One day, sure, we might plan for the long term. For now, we loved each other's families, kept our confidences, came home most nights and watched television together, played cribbage and chess, walked our neighborhood to a restaurant or bar or café, with books or just to sit and talk, volunteered and saw friends together. We ran on the lakefront in Chicago, along the bay in Miami, and around the state buildings in Bucharest. We practiced the rituals of a marriage, and whatever our temperaments, however the reluctance, we enjoyed and found meaning in them.

But this is speaking in summary, without particulars. Here is the moment of crisis and our coming through together three times, mobile, intact, and in love. First, north of Uptown, near the Chicago lakefront, touring the larger apartment where we would live for two years. Second, in a living room in Chicago, in a moment of ultimatum. Finally, in front of the People's Palace of Bucharest, considering a job offer. Each time we are exhausted and afraid, a little older. We have talked out every detail, and now we look at each other. Katie is holding my hands and standing very close. I hate seeing her like this, as I know she hates, more than anything, feeling vulnerable. *Do we really want to do this?* she asks, and each time I know she really means, *I know how much you love me, and I love you, and still, this might not work out. This might be a terrible, terrible mistake. And once we make it, we will not be able to walk it back, not really, not without consequences.* And I will pause a moment, because I think it is rude not to seem to consider the question, but I know my answer. I will say, without hesitation, *Yes.*

The ruby is more precious than the opal, and the rose gold is a higher quality than the white, but the opal ring is the one I like to take out and admire. It means our beginning. The pale blue has an aspect that changes with the light, sometimes green and yellow, at other times almost silver. I like thinking about the basement jeweler on Michigan Avenue and how close I felt then to my sister-in-law as we agreed Katie would like an opal best. I think that one day I will give this ring to one of Katie's nieces when she marries, and she will wear it in Katie's memory and be happy.

For now, I keep the opal ring and the ruby. The box remains in a state of process, changing with time, perhaps—like Katie's thin wedding band—to one day go missing and become lost.

I keep the box. I will not give away the rest of these last few things that belonged to Katie and me. They will mean something else eventually, to whoever inherits or discovers them. And perhaps it is best to invent the connections between the dull and beautiful objects, to imagine the particulars rather than try to understand them. After all, they might mean nothing. Mere tchotchkes, curios—all the debris of a life—magnified and elaborated to a grief more clear than the corresponding life itself.

Widowhood is the final carry-forward remainder of our marriage, the sequence of numbers that refuse to resolve in multiples or factors that mark a gap between what is remembered and what was lived. In the minds of many who loved Katie, long after her death, I remained Katie's husband. Even after I lost the marriage, I took a great deal of pride in being her husband.

Mid-October we flew into Milwaukee from Miami, rented a car, and drove southwest toward Moline, where Dave and Meghan would marry. Coming down I-94 we missed the interchange at Tomah and followed a series of back roads that paralleled soybeans and cornfields. Two teenagers in a Subaru told us that any left would take us to the highway. An hour later we were unsure if we would ever find the exit. Embankments, then gas stations, more cities: Ithaca, Lewiston, Rock Island, Ipava, Itasca, Ottawa. Losing the Chicago radio stations, Katie cycled through our CDs. We had no idea how much farther to Moline. Every time Katie restarted *A Man Ain't Made of Stone*, I remembered more of the lyrics. While Dave and Meghan practiced their vows, we sat in the car singing "Digging Up Bones" and "Forever and Ever, Amen." The next day we danced at Dave and Meghan's wedding. I was an usher at their ceremony. After the toasts and cake, we said our goodbyes and called it a night. We flew back to Miami. It was the beginning of winter, and the humidity was just breaking.

A therapist said to think of Katie's death as a story. Name the parts that are too difficult, and then leave them out. Tell the story again and again, until those difficult parts come back.

Is it easier to think of our life together as a collection of facts and events, rather than one complete, exhaustive sequence?

I'm not certain that either Katie's life or our life together had certainty and coherence; that how we lived was exactly the one life described in eulogies and tributes, with its tidy beginning, middle, and end, full of premature accomplishment. Katie's death magnified her ambitious life and rounded off its edges. She died, as many people said, *doing what she loved*. Had we lived together another year, another ten years, another fifty—had Katie lived at all—our time together, whatever its conclusion, might have all seemed a rather minor preamble.

Only one perspective carries forward: my own. Katie can no more refute my account after her death than put forward her own. But she left a partial defense. In her journals Katie wrote regularly about her own sense of uncertainty. Could she be the wife I wanted? Why was our timing always off? Would we ever have children? Among descriptions of daily life, frustrations with work and family, records of jogs and yoga sessions, her perspective on marriage alternates reluctance and faith, self-doubt and self-recrimination. How hard she must have worked to meet me halfway, given all of her uncertainty. Then, I didn't know to feel gratitude for it. Now, I cannot thank her. I knew that Katie felt uncertain about the institution of marriage and, sometimes, our own marriage. This part always came forward in fights and conversations. I had no idea— was I not listening? did I not want to hear it?—she judged herself so harshly for the critique.

Young Americans

1.

Before Katie's death, I saw our beginning clearly. I told the story about dancing at a party in Dhaka, both of us a little drunk and each of us saying something clever. I described the bus ride that next month and my taking the empty seat next to hers; how Katie pulled my arm over her and leaned into me so matter-of-factly that when my arm fell asleep I did not move it, not even as I lost feeling into the shoulder, so that we might keep talking about the families, hometowns, and friends back home we would most likely never meet, imagining ourselves and our lives in enough detail that we seemed to know each other instantly. Dinner the next night in

Dhaka. The park where we finally noticed the security guard watching us. The morning a mutual friend looked at Katie's neck and said, *Man, this hangover sucks harder than Big John.*

I tell myself now that I will not reanimate a ghost; that if the fact of Katie's death ends our life together, then I can make no sequence of events that does not also initiate tragedy. Why begin with optimism a story that must dissemble reluctance and violence?

There is a competing claim to this logic, a way of making the past that seeks emphasis and invention, rather than sequence. Say it is the difference between closing down every possibility into some broad lie, on the one hand, and finding instead the feeling, however disjointed, that makes the senseless and violent end of a life something more deeply felt than the trivial anecdote of its sensational facts. Before Katie's death, I would not think to make a distinction between how our life began and how the feeling of the marriage was invented and sustained. I didn't have to make the distinction. The fact of our marriage, not Katie's death, was the decisive moment of our life together.

It feels good to tell an exceptional story about us, one that makes certain virtues essential—selflessness, service, privation—in unlikely places no one we knew had visited or was likely to visit. *Katie and I were Peace Corps volunteers who fell in love in Bangladesh, made a life in Chicago and Miami, and then went abroad one last time to Romania, where we lived for the last year of her life.* In such a story, we arrive, always, at another place. We are young, idealistic, selfless, hard-working. We are an idea of ourselves, fixed in that time, which is now lost forever.

What were we doing in the middle of Bangladesh? We were dating. We were serving our country and changing lives. Bangladesh *isn't real*; we said this to each other constantly. We lived in sparse, cement-walled rooms rented from our schools. We took buses, rickshaws, and two-cycle motor taxis to leave them. Smog made our phlegm black. Red circles marked wells drilled into arsenic. We tested our water and carried it in ten-gallon plastic barrels from the well to the front gate of our schools, where we taught hygiene classes and met with local politicians, who drew phonetic squares and drilled the z and j sounds.

Zack drives John to the zoo in his Jeep.
Joe jokes that Zahir zings the xylophone.

My students said I looked and sounded like President Clinton: tall, young, and midwestern, with blond hair and thick-rimmed glasses. To them all Americans looked the same. When President Clinton visited that spring on his last world tour in office, the entire Peace Corps contingent stood in a cluster opposite the runway, watching Air Force One and waiting to greet him. We shook the hands of senators and aides as his procession arrived at the airport. President Clinton wore a new suit that afternoon, blue with a gold tie, tailored by a local Bangladeshi. He was leonine, wary. He looked each of us in the eye, and somehow he knew to stop and ask the volunteer from Arkansas where she had gone to high school. We smiled and cheered. Then, he was gone, up the stairwell, which rolled into a larger cargo plane further down the runway. Plane after plane disappeared into the night sky. Wouldn't we leave Bangladesh so gracefully?

In the beginning, when I hadn't seen Katie for a few weeks, her face seemed sharper than it did the last time, her eyes a different blue. There was nuance in her voice, her laugh round and smooth in a way that I didn't quite remember. Had her front teeth always had that gap? Was that scar over her left or right eye? Always, one of us had gained or lost weight. Katie wore raw silk and a hand-sewn cotton shalwar in public, covering her face, making her body shapeless. Sometimes I heard her voice before I saw her mouth. I thought of it as running the dub on a video: trying to synch words with lips. The effect lasted only a few minutes, but I remember thinking it was strange, that I could imagine someone so vividly in her absence that she might seem to become someone else.

The Peace Corps was a finishing school, a nondenominational cult, a secular house of worship. We spoke in acronyms—RPCV, PST, IST, PCMO, APCD—that meant we lived on the other side of the world, where the water was not clean, the roads were not paved, and the people were impressed by our relative size. All of this distinction required a separate and secret code of efficient communication. Americans were tall and well fed. We nourished babies that thrived. On the walls of our rooms were photographs of handsome, wealthy people: family members, in fact, who lived in our family homes.

When the Peace Corps conducted official business, its representatives arrived in enormous sport-utility vehicles, with tinted windows and chrome grills across the headlights. Officers and staff members in crisp shirts and bland ties wore expensive watches and, always, sunglasses. They broke into sweats immediately, because their cars in the monsoon heat had been cooled for hours to artic temperatures. But they spoke the language. They drank whatever was offered them. In this way the Peace Corps was an ideal, an argument, a mobile promised land working a methodical, slow reveal. We volunteers were its prophets, the elect ambassadors who made our country beautiful by example. We carried backpacks and wore sandals, but everyone seemed to understand that if we were threatened, a battalion of marines would arrive instantly and extract us into the sky.

Katie applied to the Peace Corps, she said, because she hated hearing John Lennon and Yoko Ono's "Happy Christmas! (War Is Over)" in shopping malls, at holiday parties, and especially late at night, by request, when she delivered pizzas in the Twin Cities. Why was the song following her, and what did it want from her? She didn't know. She was not doing enough to help the world, she believed, because if she was doing enough, then John Lennon and Yoko Ono would not hound her to do more.

I applied to the Peace Corps, I told her, because everyone I admired at my university was applying to the Peace Corps. It was a process to begin that took more than a year to complete, becoming more elaborate and specific with each successive interview, medical exam, and clearance, until the selected were understood to be, in every way, exceptional. I loved the sense of momentum and possibility. The experience and destination would change me, I agreed. I could think of it only in the abstract, how my time in the Peace Corps might make me vital and return me home transformed.

It did not matter which region of the world I helped or whether I could locate it on a map. The country to which I was originally assigned, Mongolia, could very well have been the same country where I ultimately served, Bangladesh. I did not know the difference among Central Asia, South Asia, and Southeast Asia. In my naïve mind it was one giant amorphous movie set: rice paddy, monsoon, distant Himalaya. I believed that I would arrive anywhere on the globe and immediately solve problems. I was a young American abroad. The Peace Corps told me it was likely I would not only help people but also love doing so.

In the weeks after Katie's death, I felt that same uncertain inclination to optimism about a person I might one day become. I had plenty of opportunities to practice being that person, in public and private gatherings that honored Katie. In Bucharest Katie's coworkers laid fresh flowers at her desk. A colleague spoke about Katie's sacrifice to save lives the night she died and how her doing so followed the life of service she led in Romania and America. An icon of the Virgin Mary was presented by an Orthodox priest. I was given cake and wine to bring home to Katie's family. When it was my turn to speak, I tried to say something about how our last day on that hike together had been ideal; how Katie loved to hike, and to be outdoors with friends, and she had spent a full day doing both; that I had loved doing those things with Katie and also seeing her so happy. I wanted to thank those colleagues for remembering her so well, and I also wanted to make their memory of us certain. How could we ever forget Katie's spirit, I said, her generosity, smile, and laughter? How would we live after her?

A week later, in Illinois, I laid over Katie's ashes flowers from the fifty-odd bouquets at her funeral mass. Katie's mom and I drank the bottle of wine. The outfit I picked for Katie's cremation was ordinary, even familiar: the khaki pants and blue button-down she wore most days to work. I had thought briefly to have the body dressed head-to-toe in soft fleece. To see her in them would have meant she was warm and happy. I couldn't do it. I was dressing Katie for the journey that would bring her home. I resolved myself to the ritual, thinking, *This is another opportunity to honor Katie's life.*

An hour before I stood with Katie's family in the funeral home in her hometown, I took two small, white, oblong pills. I was terrified to do the wrong thing in front of so many people. Rather than break down in public, I wanted to feel nothing. I meant to become the indistinct mourner, onto whom hundreds of well-intentioned strangers could project their well-meaning comfort. In this way I did not have to feel anything myself. I could stand dumb and silent, smiling at everyone, trying to say something polite about the best parts of Katie's life.

2.

Katie and I married on a Saturday, at the beginning of spring, during the first weekend of apple blossom season. We hired covered wagons for hayrides and took wedding photos on a giant show tractor, walking under a trellis, in a lofted barn strung with tea lights. Friends and family ate freshly baked cookies, dancing to a sing-along of Dylan's "Forever Young." We walked down the aisle to Iris Dement's "Let the Mystery Be." Our wedding party was our three nieces, my brother, Ed, and my cousin Wayne. Friends handmade invitations and ran the sound system. Another friend took photographs. The meal was buffet style, a do-it-yourself burrito bar with homemade guacamole and salsa, a keg of Leinenkugel's, and a Rubbermaid bin filled with sangria. Toward the end of the night a friend topped an empty 7Up two-liter bottle with sangria and ran around the dance floor, insisting everyone take swigs. Ed wrote new lyrics to "Sweet Violets," one of Katie's father's favorite songs, and sang it with his kids.

Katie and I had no particular connection to the County Line Orchard in Hobart, Indiana. It was a good middle point for guests arriving in Chicago and Indianapolis, near an airport, with decent hotels. The previous night, after the rehearsal, my father had held court in the hotel lobby bar, buying rounds of drinks for our guests. A friend from high school told stories. Another friend made toasts. Table to table, cheers went up as Katie and I crossed each other, seeking out still other friends to greet and thank. We were festive. *Here was the end*, I thought, *to that part of our lives we had made separately*, the last time we would tend to some part without each other. We gathered everyone we loved to one place, with all of their good wishes, to witness it.

Katie's friends from college were married now. Some had babies. Others were just pregnant, or trying, or looking into adoption programs, filling out forms, waiting. A few owned apartments or houses. Would we settle down now? they asked. We said we were traveling light and seeing what came our way. We would pack boxes that next week, load up the moving truck, and head out for a new home in Florida. We thanked everyone as we continued to pass through.

In wedding photos Katie's face is smooth and bright. She rarely wore makeup, so the effect is the startling and unfamiliar exaggeration of her features. We look like any white, midwestern, middle-class couple, and I suppose this is how we meant to present ourselves for posterity: smiling and poised. After our kiss at the end of the ceremony, Katie hugged me tight, and when she pulled away there was a pale stain across the front of my suit jacket.

3.

By a coincidence of missed buses and late flights Katie and I spent the evening of September 11, 2001, watching television in Dhaka. A friend called from another room in the hostel to say the Pentagon and World Trade Centers were on fire. For the next twenty hours we only watched television. We could not leave the capital until we received the all-clear from the Peace Corps office, which was busy leaving phone messages for volunteers in all of the other cities, then calling our families back home to say we were safe. We waited to hear that we were all accounted for, the embassy was secure, and we might soon return to the place where we had worked and lived for two years. We spoke to each other in reassuring tones. We waited for direction.

Everything, the commentators on the television keep explaining, *will now be very different.*

In our small room no one seemed exactly certain how to measure either the quality or the scope of the impending change. When we could not keep watching television, we watched movies. The cable movie channels did not interrupt their programming, so we caught the end of a comedy, then a war epic, then a musical. We did not want to sleep. How could we? Our country was in immediate peril. HBO was showing a Robert De Niro marathon. When we could not stay inside our room any longer, we tried to decide together whether it was safe to leave the hostel. Were terrorists waiting in the lobby to kill us? If not, could we buy chicken schwarma at this hour? Dhaka seemed suddenly hostile to our presence. As we walked through the neighborhood, life was distinctly unaware of us: the price of rice unchanged, televisions turned to cricket matches.

A few weeks later, the night before we were evacuated from Bangladesh, Katie and I packed what we could fit into our backpacks and left our sites on the last night buses. Whoever came to find us that next morning arrived at half-abandoned rooms strewn with papers and stacked with clothes, photographs, cassette tapes, and books. We hoped it seemed, for a while at least, only that we had forgotten to take out our trash and clean our kitchens.

We left Bangladesh for Bangkok. We flew from South Asia to Korea, took a discount tour of China, and finally landed at my parents' home for the holiday. After Thanksgiving we flew one last time, to Chicago, where we both found work. I was a middle school social studies teacher. Katie managed the office of a green-development nonprofit. I slept most nights at Katie's studio sublet in Lincoln Park, until after a while I had my own key, laundry pile, and grocery list. Evenings, we ran along the lakefront to one of the beaches and back. We came home, showered, made dinner, and played chess, cribbage, and rummy.

Wasn't this our new, ordinary, and immodest life? Everything in America seemed luxuriously indulgent. We took buses and trains that ran on time and arrived a few blocks from heated offices. My Chicago public school classroom had its own telephone line and internet connection, a mobile computer lab in the back of the room, and several five-pound bags of candy in a locked storage cabinet. Sometimes, in the middle of the day, I sent Katie an instant message on the computer, and she wrote instantly back.

I like my job!

I like my job, too!

For the first time in either of our lives, we saved money. We opened checking accounts and savings accounts. We subscribed to magazines and theater seasons, took dance lessons, and traveled weekends to visit our families. Tuesdays and Saturdays the diner across the street served four pancakes, a fried egg, and three sausage links, with pie and coffee, for six dollars. Movie rentals were two-for-one four nights a week.

Those evenings we spent in the apartment, Katie wore fleece sweatpants and made tea. She curled herself onto the ridiculous yellow-leather loveseat we inherited from previous tenants, to read books and magazines. I put my head in her lap, or we lay on the bed with the windows open, the cat teetering on the sill as we listened to the traffic, turning our pages. When it was hot in the city, we pulled the mattress under the window or set up the laptop to watch hours of television into the afternoon and evening. We liked to argue about whether the cat's indifference to the traffic below meant she was charmed or incredibly stupid. I defended the cat vigorously. *Survival of the fittest*, Katie liked to say, *when her time is up, her time is up.*

4.

It is a warm June evening in Bucharest. The beer gardens and pizza shops around Bucharest's enormous Lake Herastrau, which one side of our apartment building overlooks, are just open for the season. Someone is selling flowers from an umbrella stand: neon carnations mixed with weeds and grasses.

We walk the loop again and again around the lake.

Bucharest is by far our favorite city yet, and like every other city in which we have lived together, we intend to leave it with a sense that we have only just begun our explorations. We are excellent planners, even when we have no goal. Katie is starting yoga classes again and going with her friend to the gym. She is exercising to manage work-related stress. Membership in a private gym is a status symbol among the city's elite. Bucharest is filled with families that have profited wildly and handsomely after Communism, privatizing industry, franchising corporations, dumping Western

Europe's toxic waste in parts unknown of the Carpathian Mountains. Much of Katie's work puts her in daily contact with terrible people who have real power and speak fluent English. Katie swims laps with their charming families in the morning and then walks past their offices on her way to work.

Katie will die in six weeks, but of course we cannot know this. We do not plan for it. We walk nearly every night around Lake Herastrau, complaining that we are bored, restless, and eager to explore still more beer gardens, park benches, trees, dams, and apartment buildings on either side with the avenues and the traffic circles between them. What else can we do until it is time, finally, to leave? We entertain ourselves. We people-watch. Romanians out walking, mostly kids, intermix family with youthful, libertarian élan. We have neither community nor zeal. It doesn't really matter. We find the end of one conversation and begin the next. We repeat our conversations as we circle the lake. Every few hundred yards we pass a restaurant blaring British rock music: the Rolling Stones and Queen, Sid Vicious singing "My Way" and David Bowie singing "Young Americans." It is the music of liberation and exhaustion, and we are lost.

5.

I stand in a small field at our Peace Corps training site. The coordinator has chalked an outline of Bangladesh onto the grass. As we each receive our assignment, we take the placard on which it is written and straddle our city. I get "Tangail," a city the travel guide calls "the singularly least attractive place in Bangladesh." It is a transportation hub across which the local crime syndicate taxes buses and cars as they make their way north from and south to the capital. Tangail's de facto leader is recently imprisoned for beating a police officer to death with the leg of a stool, at the police station, while in police custody. He is reputed to have a violent temper. After his release, at his request, I teach his wife English.

The afternoon I receive my assignment, I smile like everyone else as we take a group photograph. Katie is fifteen, maybe twenty feet away, with five volunteers stationed in the cities between our cities. In the photograph I can just make out her dark hair and blue head scarf in the middle of the group. The coordinator walks across the map to congratulate each of us. He explains that he has picked me for Tangail because the Peace Corps needs *someone really large there*. It is a hard assignment, he says, but he knows I will do it well.

I think, *All of that training, and here is the criteria for my advantage, relative size.*

Even now I consider the choice again and what I think it means my time in Bangladesh might become. I try to imagine the life that follows, getting every part of the sequence wrong. How does falling in love with Katie start with this moment? How can our meeting here end years later in Romania with her death?

If I am ironic, then I say the next two years will contain the useless and immensely gratifying skill of smashing dying cockroaches, of learning when they are at their most vulnerable in my small cement room or already almost dead.

If I am earnest, then I speak thoughtfully about how a tragedy in one part of the world magnified our sense of need and commitment, until suddenly Katie and I were traveling the world together.

How can I not want to enter that sequence again and again, so that I might disrupt it?

I tell this part of the story because it hedges against larger and less certain speculations—boredom, order, meaning—and misses, always, the improbabilities of coincidence and scale.

I can walk our life together back this far: I am well-intentioned, naïve, and unambitious. I can find my life in the consequence of one decision and very little before it. I hardly think about the decision, over which I have control and influence. My role is consequent and representative. I'm not sure I have a right to contest it.

I do not want to seem disagreeable. I thank the country director as he walks across the country to congratulate someone else.

6.

Is it resignation, then, that ends my witness of the beginning of our marriage? Confusion? A certainty of arriving at, then becoming acted upon and overwhelmed by, a repeating pattern of circumstance and place? How closely that story follows my witness of Katie's death, her funeral, and my continuing life in Indiana, where everyone quickly learns some version of that sequence. I move to Indiana with the celebrity and mystery of yet another country visited, and once again, I assemble a life in the aggregate and from a distance.

What should I do, then, with these last parts of the memory of our life together? The disparate pieces that seem to no longer belong to the whole? Picking Katie up at the last bus from campus. Working a Bon Jovi concert to raise money for a charity. Eating tacos at the truck by her office in Chicago.

Can I assemble them into anything worth saying?

One spring we trained together for a marathon. We ran six, eight, twelve miles a day, and when Katie turned her ankle and stopped running, still she followed me sometimes on her bike, calling out my split times, making small talk.

Can't I prove we were in love, happy, committed, special?

I see no contract with our past selves. It was too easy to arrive in a new city and begin the process of restarting a life. Unpacking boxes. Mapping out the route to work. Finding grocery stores and learning the words for chicken, apple, rice, coffee. No part of our life then says we teetered on any brink. Why should it? We were volunteers, teachers, and young Americans. We were married, and soon we would work abroad again. We had graduate degrees, ambitions, résumés. When Katie died, we were traveling into the mountains, on vacation, between cities.

I will resist the lie that both story and affection must entirely transform in order to survive after her death. I will try again to tell the beginning, as I might have told it before Katie's death, a beginning that is false and irrelevant and that perhaps stretches too easily its surfaces across a life. Isn't this the consolation I seek from anecdotes: to suggest, in the place of feeling, reverence? To adapt a practice of faith, confession, to the secular realm? In devotion to see Katie more clearly and our marriage in its former, more perfect light?

7.

The new country director, arriving from Boston, held a welcome party for all of the volunteers at his rented home in Dhaka. There was a deejay, fried American foods, cold beer, and cake. Everyone made toasts. At the end of the night, Katie and I danced together, and when the song ended, she looked up at me. We were both a little drunk.

John Evans, she said, *how come we don't spend more time together?*
I smiled. I loved moments like this.
Because, Katie LaPlante, I said, *you can't stand me.*

The Legend of a Life

1. The Jesus Rock

Katie had arranged a surprise for my birthday the next week. All during the hike, she enjoyed teasing me about it. Playing along, I asked for a hint.

It is something that you don't enjoy until you see it, but then you are very happy.

She pushed ahead to find Sara.

I take five short videos of our group that day. In no particular sequence we stand in front of a waterfall a third of the way up the trail. We hold our breaths a moment; our faces are lean and full of hesitation, our voices higher pitched than I remember. When we relax into ourselves the image captures a certain fleeting bonhomie of the day, the good intentions of our being together. We alternately smile and clown, joking that we hope the photo looks good.

Of course, these are not photos. Each time I press the wrong button. We pose. Someone says there is no flash; the green light isn't blinking. Our camera records thirty frames per second: 180 to 300 photographs with each failed take. Each video is so broad and inclusive as to emphasize nothing. The frame is too grainy. There is some kind of delay in how the camera pans that makes the image choppy. Perhaps, in more capable hands, the potential for extraction would exceed the wealth of data. To me it is all a blur.

This is our group in every lost photograph: Katie, me, Sara, and three strangers we met that morning at the base of the mountain, who agreed to join us for the long hike and with whom we become fast friends for the day. The Israeli couple on honeymoon has backpacked across Eastern Europe all summer. Friendly and very fit, seeming very much in love, they chose Busteni for its easy access into the Carpathians. She is a doctor who works at a hospital in Tel Aviv. He has some vague association with the military that no one seems eager to clarify. I tease Sara about it constantly, knowing she is paranoid about such things. The Romanian, the last member of our group, is hiking, at least in part, to kill his massive hangover. We have all talked a bit that morning, sitting together in the small waiting room next to the cable cars that never begin— high winds, early morning rain—the day's run up the mountain. Now, we have all agreed to set off together up the nearby hiking trails.

These videos are the last record I have of Katie's voice. She will die in six hours, and she does not mean to be recorded. She is saying nothing in particular, and later I will think, *This is how I remem-*

ber the sound of her voice now. *I cannot exactly recall it. I hear it in
echoes, always just before or after the thing I am remembering, as though
she is not talking to me.*

Katie hikes ahead with Sara for a while and then falls back with the
Romanian. He struggles to keep the pace. Katie is a natural athlete
and leader, she has a terrific capacity for empathy—all of this is
true—but she also understands that he is slowing down the group,
so she hikes with him to keep us moving together up the mountain. We wait at river crossings and outcrops. He is overweight,
winded. He explains to Katie that he works for an electronics firm
in Bucharest and was out the night before partying at a club. The
hike is more strenuous than he imagined it might be, as it was, more
and more, for all of us.

I keep a steady place in the middle of the pack with the Israeli
couple. We stop at an alpine face and climb single-file across a short
distance using a pull rope, keeping our bodies flat as we move sideways across the rock. It is the hardest part of the hike, but we can
see the end of the trail once we have crossed halfway: a giant white
cross perched at the edge of the land, running its midday shadow
dramatically down our path.

Later, we take photos in front of that cross and then behind its
shadow, which stretches ten or fifteen feet at an angle from the
ridge, widening to a peak. The Israelis like the spot. I use their camera to take thirty-two digital shots of them posing near it. It is hard
to get the sense of scale right, and it is late in the day, so the angle
drifts in each photograph, as though the shadow is following us,
or we are approaching it from every direction. We have hiked all
day to the top of the mountain, watching the shadow of the cross
for the last part of the way.

A small snack stand waits where the path levels out onto the ridge,
an old cabin in which someone has thought to prospect the for-

tunes of desperate, self-congratulating hikers. We buy candy bars and cold sodas. Katie and the Romanian arrive last, and after a while Katie asks me to walk with her a ways further, separate from the group.

I found a rock with the face of Jesus on it.

She smiles nervously and laughs. I laugh, too.

I hiked ahead and saw it on the ground.

Don't worry, though. I rubbed the mud a little, and the face disappeared.

We walk back to the snack stand and open sodas. I shake out rocks from my shoes, put on a sweater, and lie down on one of the benches to catch my breath.

It is beautiful on the ridge. There is a pile of rocks down which snow melts into a small river across it. The sun is out and closer now to the horizon. It was warm in Bucharest, but here on the ridge it is windy and cold.

We decide we should keep moving, find food, and rent rooms for the night. There is a small hostel just to our right, but it does not have a kitchen. So we hike another mile or so across level terrain, to a larger hostel whose dining room, the guidebook says, looks out over a valley, toward the sunset.

The larger hostel where we eat dinner is crowded with summer tourists stuck at the top of the mountain, waiting all day for the cable cars. Of course, the tourists in the hotel cannot leave the mountain; they have been stranded in the hostel all night and day. They are keeping their rooms and staying at least until morning. The kitchen is nearly running on bare provisions. We eat pickled vegetables and a broth soup with stale bread and cold beer.

The Israelis keep insisting that we start back across the ridge toward the smaller hostel, to rent a room for the night. But the rest of the group isn't worried, and we say as much. It is getting late, and soon it will be dark. The path is a little less than a mile across level terrain. We ask the Romanian to call ahead to the smaller hostel on the house phone. We are grateful that someone in our group speaks Romanian well enough to work out the details. There is one room left, the owner explains, and we can claim it if we arrive within the hour.

Back out on the trail, Katie sits down suddenly, grimaces, and begins to cry. She has turned her ankle on a rock. I sit a while with her, until she feels strong enough to keep walking. I offer to help, but she insists that the ankle is fine: she just wants to hang back from the rest of the group with Sara by the lake, under the stars. They will follow in time. We should go ahead and be sure to get the room.

Do you need an ice pack? Should I ask the hostel for a first-aid kit so that we can wrap it?

Katie hates doctors. She understands her injury. She first rolled her ankle six years earlier, while we were hiking in South Korea, at the trailhead coming down Mount Daegu. She insisted on walking on it to reach the bus back to the city and later refused medical attention, eating handfuls of ibuprofen for the next few days, until the swelling went down a little and the color came back. It was only a year later, after the ankle started to click and swell whenever we went running in Chicago, that a doctor diagnosed a fracture that had not healed correctly. The clicking was the sound of the joint rubbing against itself. The ankle would swell like that, the doctor explained, whenever she turned it.

I am mad at Katie for staying back, for turning her ankle, and for letting the injury persist when she knows she loves to run and hike. I think she is foolish to insist on resting by herself now, to not let me help her. It is only a sprained ankle, but we still have the mile to hike. And, it is late.

But I also know that part of me is relieved to do nothing, to be absolved of any obligation to help her, to keep going and leave her stubbornness behind. We have been hiking all day. I am tired. I do not want to pick the fight.

Suit yourself.

Which is the last memory I have of Katie, alive and well: my saying goodbye with a great harrumph, leaving her on a hill with Sara and the Romanian.

There is a photo of Katie and me standing that evening under the kilometer marker next to the lake, with the rocks to the right and behind us. You can see water coming off the ridge, and if you look closely enough, you can just make out an outline of snow and ice where the white rocks darken under the clouds. I am wearing a Cubs hat, plaid shorts, and a black sweater. Katie is wearing blue jeans, her backpack, and a t-shirt from the 5K race in her home-town. We are leaning into each other and smiling. I have pursed my lips into the kind of pseudo-smile-and-smirk I once imagined demonstrated great thoughtfulness and consideration, perhaps poetic resignation.

We are standing on a tall mountain in Romania. Yes, we are.

Katie is exhausted, still in pain, and smiling through her teeth. She smiles this way when she is smiling against her better judg-ment. I remember thinking it was important to get this picture right. It would be a kind of evidence to friends and family of our ridiculous day of hiking.

Sara takes the photograph, then hands me the camera. I step closer and photograph the two of them facing in the opposite direction, across the ridge. They are surrounded by blue sky and green land. Katie is smiling naturally. You can see it especially around her eyes. Her face is centered in the photograph. Sara is standing to her right, and a sliver of her body and face is cropped out of the frame. Her head is tilted back, as though she is laughing at a joke; perhaps it is an ironic laugh. Katie, with her blue eyes and dark features. Sara, with her Irish ruddiness, hazel eyes, and spectacular long red hair. Katie has tied a dark blue bandanna in her hair. Sara has tied a light blue bandanna around her neck. To their left three or four valleys roll in succession away from the sunset.

We purchased the bandannas at the train station that morning, on a whim, as a gesture of solidarity.

We are beginning a vacation together. We have pennants!

I am exhausted from the hike and feeling short. I am eager for our wilderness adventure to end. I am not, by either birthright or practice, much of an outdoorsman. I have arthritic toes that surgery two years earlier only made worse. It hurts to step at an incline, duck and crouch under branches, jump across rocks. I wear sneakers constantly, with an orthotic, and neither does much to help with the pain or range of motion. The trail is unmarked where the hike becomes difficult. I am out of shape. We do not have much water. I am carrying a backpack packed for the week. I am scared and exhausted. I do not like wilderness adventures, and when we push ahead, up the mountain, toward an uncertain destination; when Katie stops to rest and tells me to go ahead, I want to keep going because I want to find the end. The peak, summit, ridge, and smaller hostel. Late afternoon, evening, nightfall, sleep.

Katie is smiling in her photograph with Sara, and I think it might be a kind of *fuck you* for the day. Or, perhaps, the smile is unchanged in both photographs. In our photograph my arm is draped across Katie's shoulder. Her hair is sun-sweet. I can smell her powder-scented deodorant, shampoo, soap. I love these smells, and they are familiar. I stand there. I hear a voice telling me to look stoic. It is the end of a journey. We are victorious.

It is something that you don't enjoy until you see it, but then you are very happy.

Later that week my friend Ben forwards me the email from Katie. His plan was to come to Romania from Egypt, where he lived and worked, to celebrate my thirtieth birthday. Katie had spent the last few weeks arranging his flights, accommodations, and pickup. Sara would meet him at the airport, and Katie would make some excuse to divert me to her apartment. Ben would arrive with Sara, followed by friends from the school where I taught.

So, it was a game. There would be a winner and a loser. Or, really, at the end we would both win.

I left Katie behind with Sara because I wanted her to plan my birthday surprise; I was being generous; I was exhausted, and my feet hurt; our journey was almost finished; I did not want to disagree with her; I was angry with her; I would not indulge her injury-denying heroics; she should let me help her; we needed to claim our rooms for the night.

The truth is I left Katie behind on the trail because I imagined our life was very ordinary, invulnerable to trauma and tragedy. I understood the situation well enough to trust it. There was the predictable aspect and, always just lagging behind it, calamity. We would keep ahead of calamity because we always did. The Israelis and I would walk ahead until Sara and Katie and the fat, slow Romanian closed the gap and caught up. I would wait for them at the river crossing, where I could afford to sulk and feel petty. There was a range of ordinary possibilities, I told myself, to what would happen next.

2. Arête

The bear that killed Katie had white fur on its paws and muzzle, and for a little less than an hour it flashed white across the path of my flashlight, making a deliberate measure of her body and slowly, without pretense, pressing her chest into the ground until it made no sound and did not return the force.

This is how Katie died: gross thoracic trauma. Her body, mauled. The body, when we recovered it, bloodless and blank. It did not appear to be mangled. We stood together over her and thought she might have had a shock. She lay at an angle on the grass, and her body was intact, her clothes were not torn, there was not so much blood as we might have expected. To look at Katie's body, we thought she had survived the attack, or perhaps the attack had only happened in our imaginations, or to someone else, or someplace else.

An hour earlier my group had left Katie's group at the lake and walked a few hundred yards ahead down the path. We reached the river, where the Israeli doctor said we should wait to cross as a group. Or, her husband said, I could wait for Katie, Sara, and the Romanian while they went ahead to the smaller hostel. I watched them disappear into the darkness. I wound the mechanical charger on my flashlight, thinking that when Katie arrived I would need to show the way across. After a while, I became impatient, and then, after a longer while, concerned. What was taking them so long? I called Katie, then Sara on their cell phones. I left long, insistent messages to which they never listened, encouraging them to pick up the pace.

Perhaps, I thought much later, *the ringing of her cell phone angered the bear and inspired it to take a second pass across the ridge.*

I turned back to the path and after several false starts found my way to the lake. They were not there. I screamed Katie's name, then Sara's into the night wind; I could not remember the Romanian's name. It was still louder now, but there were gaps in the wind when I could make my voice distinct.

Just across the path I saw what looked like clumps of feathers on the gravel. I reached down and picked up the pages from our guidebook, ripped from the spine and torn in half. I turned the crank and shined my light down into the brook. Had someone from Katie's group fallen into the water? Had they all slipped on the rocks? The rocks sloped down to the river at an angle. If a person fell sideways toward the stream, I thought, they might lose consciousness, bleed, even drown. I tried to move faster and climb down to the stream, but I could make very little progress in the dark.

I turned the flashlight crank and tried to make broad sweeps of the water. I climbed back to the trail and yelled Katie's name again. Somehow I had turned myself around, because now I was facing out opposite both the smaller and the larger hostel, toward the ridge we had kept to our right as we crossed. It was then that I heard Katie's voice and swung my flashlight around. I saw nothing, but I heard her:

Don't come closer. Find a gun. Get back quickly.

Perhaps my screaming voice and Katie's response, after so much silence, made the bear curious, even irritated to understand what he had happened upon, at being unable to synchronize his poor eyesight with the urgent noise.

In a moment, in the ten minutes it took me to reach the smaller hostel and plead with the hostel owner to take his rifle, Katie would be alone on the ridge. First, the Romanian would sit up and punch at the bear, wildly, shrieking and screaming, and when the bear turned away, he would run toward the hostel's porch light. The bear would not follow him. Sara would later say she did not know why she also sat up and screamed and ran. She had no memory of leaving Katie, only of seeing the lamp swinging from the porch of the smaller hostel, and then it getting larger as she, too, ran, screaming and crying, toward it.

I remember all of this in the reverse order. Sara coming down the path, out of the darkness, distraught. The Romanian, already inside of the smaller hostel when I arrived, rocking under a blanket, saying only that he had managed to get away. I remember thinking, *Katie cannot be far behind,* because if Sara—urban, neurotic, slight—could survive the attack, then surely, so too would Katie. I remember thinking, with some hope, *If the fat Romanian survived, then Katie must already be here.* I had only to wait a little longer on the porch.

Then, I was arguing with the hostel owner. He had a rifle, he explained, but he could not let me take it. He would be fined forty thousand Romanian lire for discharging a gun without a state permit to do so. All of the guests were witnesses. His business would be ruined. Two strangers—his sons? other tourists?—held my arms back, and a third stood between us. I thought, *It is important that I try to get the gun,* and I knew I would not get it. I offered him American dollars, my passport, my pack. I thought, *All of this is taking too long.* Someone else said to wait in the hostel until we knew there was no bear and I thought, *This is when I should be heroic and go save Katie.* I staggered out the door and toward the path. Time was slowing down now. It took forever to hike back up the trail and find Katie again. I thought, *There will be a funeral at the church and a newspaper report and I will have to give a speech and I will need to bring the body home to Katie's mother and someone else will have to ship the cats,* and I hated myself for thinking it through so thoroughly.

I could not run and keep my footing. When I found the place again, Katie had been alone there for twenty, maybe twenty-five minutes. Now, she was dying. I was sure of it from the sound of her voice and the manner of the bear: deliberate, certain, indifferent to my arrival. It was *doing* something. It had a sense of purpose. It did not retreat, even when the rocks I threw struck its fur and hindquarters.

I thought, *The bear will turn toward me because I am provoking it, and when it charges, I will run down the path, and it will follow me away from Katie.*

Before that night we had never seen a bear. Which does not matter now, except to say that no one, especially Katie, whom we all imagined knew exactly what to do if attacked by a bear, had an idea of encounter or survival beyond the hypothetical situation. Play dead. Wait for the bear to lose interest. Leave.

I watched the attack, trying to close the distance: fifteen, maybe twenty yards. Every time I thought to approach and intervene, I could not move my body forward. I panicked, but I also had a sense to fear for my own life. It was as though I stood on the rooftop terrace of a tall building, leaning my head to look over the side, imagining I was about to fall, while my feet remained at a distance from the ledge.

In the moment I was ashamed of myself. The shame alternated a clear-headed practicality about survival with an untested capacity for heroism that would not come forward. It felt like cowardice. I threw rocks, yelled, and waved my arms at the bear.

I thought, *The bear will lose interest if I land a large enough rock near its head, and then it will scatter.*

I had no perspective on Katie's body, except to watch the bear's muzzle dip and lift over it. It seemed to move in and out of focus, as though spot-lit for a stage performance or caught in headlights. The white fur was thickest at the paws, or perhaps I was most comfortable watching the space just in front of its body. The scene was revealed partially with what I could manage to shine and how steadily I held the light. But the sound was constant; it invited speculation. The wind, the tearing of clothes, the snorting and grunting bear, all combined like woodcuts to assemble those parts of the scene I was constantly not seeing. I could fill in the gaps only as I imagined them.

Katie screamed, at first words, then only the sound of her making noise, no longer a voice but something deep, rasped, and loud that seemed to continue out of habit, long after it might have stopped. I could not see Katie's face or the entire length of the bear. I remember imagining for a moment the cartoon shape of a bear from a children's book, overlaid on bright paper, filling the darkness with unmeasured angles.

I thought, *Why is no one coming to help me?* I moved my limbs through molasses, at the darkness.

When Katie saw the bear that would kill her, she stopped walking, threw her pack across the field, and laid flat on the ground. Sara and the Romanian explained much later that they had all made themselves small at first and spoke only in hushed tones. Katie had led this progression to the ground. Sara had also thrown her pack in the opposite direction. At first, it seemed, they acted together, certain of a survival they coordinated in hushed tones—*Stay down. Don't move*—even as the bear moved closer, taking its time, measuring the stillness around each body.

Bears in the wild are revealed, rather than seen. They are territorial by nature. They move in clans. They do not share open spaces. Rabid, startled, drunk, or hungry bears, and also cub mothers, violate these patterns. Brown bears weigh up to fifteen hundred pounds, have three-inch claws, and can run thirty miles per hour. Unlike a black bear, a brown bear on the attack rarely loses interest or spooks. Black bears lose interest when its prey plays dead; brown bears move closer.

Katie knew some of this in the moment. I think often that Katie must have been so frustrated, believing she was doing the right thing, waiting for the bear to do its part and leave. She did what an American in the wilderness is supposed to do when she sees a black bear. Katie must have felt hopeful about her survival. Perhaps she was not conscious in the moment during the attack when I arrived. Or perhaps she knew I was there and felt disappointed that I did not do more.

This is the man I married, she thought, *the one who will not save me, who loves me but cannot save me.*

I threw bigger rocks. The bear moved away, flashed its muzzle, and moved back.

A boy and his father, hiking in the opposite direction, had stopped us just past the kilometer marker on the ridge to say they had seen a bear crossing from the other direction. It could not be far from the spot where we stood. We should be careful on the ridge at night, use our flashlights, and make as much noise as possible to announce our presence and deter an attack.

Did each of us, in that moment, imagine a bear attack and our survival? Or did we shrug off his warning as improbable, full of the wrong kind of caution? How could we suddenly be in a moment of worst-case survival? We were standing together, taking pictures next to a kilometer marker. We were making our way to the only hostel on the ridge with rooms to rent for the night. We could not stay in one place. The sky was plum colored. It was cold. The wind was picking up, and already we were wearing sweaters and stocking caps to stay warm. Already, we were survivors, in our minds, the likely elect, moving in wide circles far from danger; the very improbability of an attack, its cartoonish quality in our imaginations, made the odds of our survival more certain.

As I turned the crank to keep my flashlight on the bear, I saw a group start down the trail from the hostel. I thought, *Someone is coming to save Katie*, and then, *No, someone* else *is coming to save Katie.* I yelled to Katie to wait just a little longer.

I thought, *A husband who loves his wife would have charged the bear already.*

I walked back to the path to make a signal to the group, to jump and wave my arms, but I was too early. They processed so slowly, moving together, now a rescue party, now a funeral rite, taking care with the steep rocks and riverbank. Hours seemed to pass as their flashlights inched forward.

I could not startle the bear and also wave them down. I had chosen to walk toward them, and now a distinct feeling of inconvenience bothered my sense of helplessness. In both places, the trail and near Katie, something inevitable was made to feel drawn out. Katie would die. I knew this already; I could imagine nothing else. But also I knew we had the right tools—guns, knives, reinforced cookware—to intervene and save her, if only they would hurry up. I both wanted Katie's suffering to be over and for her voice to carry on a little longer and further, just far enough to persuade the hunters to move more quickly. But if she could not be saved, then I wanted her to die quickly. I could not listen to her screaming, even from a distance.

In the end, with their guns and yelling and clanging pots, they came like a soccer club, a band of revelers, a wedding party, all noise and celebration, unmistakable and intrusive in the cold summer night air. It must have carried for miles across the ridge. I walked back to the trail and toward them, so that they would be sure to see me.

They asked, *Where is the bear?*

They were hunters arriving, someone explained, from the nearest village. We should move together in a large, loud group toward the bear and Katie's body. We moved in darkness. We moved hypothetically, uncertain of our arrival. We saw no bear, and then we saw Katie's body. I made myself walk over and look at Katie's face. I did not want to look at it. Her face was perfect: intact. Some mud on her right cheek. Her hair down across the forehead more than usual.

And then I saw it, and I understood. We shined the light onto her face, into her eyes. The Israeli doctor was there with her husband. She performed a few simple tests. Katie's pupils, she explained, were dilated and black. They did not shine back as they should. The doctor found an irregular pulse, then no feeling. It was Katie's body. It was cold. We needed to leave the ridge before the bear returned.

In the moment before the attack, Katie walked in one direction, laughing and smiling, making progress toward a light bulb hung from the porch of the smaller hostel to which only Sara and the Romanian would arrive. Now, a hunting patrol carried her body in the other direction, toward the larger hostel where we had eaten dinner. I walked behind them. I could not touch Katie now. I was terrified of her body. I could not look at it. I thought, *We are mov-*

ing your body inside where it will be safe. In the basement of the larger hostel we laid Katie's body on a tarp on the concrete and waited for the doctors.

Arête: a sharp ridge. From the Latin *arista:* ear of wheat, fish bone, spine.

I am told that a climber makes a ridge sacred with her death, that the place where Katie died locates a point of reverence for other journeys, but I do not believe it. For a while I imagined there were flowers there and a pile of stones stained at the base with her blood, but I know this is not true. I have not returned to the place to make it sacred. I can't imagine I ever will. Any marker has long since collapsed. Or it has lifted like a prayer from the place of her death and vanished somewhere along the nearby trail.

3. The Legend of a Life

Maybe the bear had been there for a while, and they did not see it until that moment: the now-lit path, wide across the ridge, coming into focus. Katie's flashlight reflecting brighter on the far rocks as she turned the crank. She stood like that a moment, testing the charge, looking in every direction for the trail. A mountaintop.

Maybe the bear was migrating with the season, seeking out less encroached-upon spaces, guarding the path for its cubs. Seasonal construction crossing this path put the bear on edge, making it more cautious but also wilder, wary. Hunters crossed here; and tourists with cameras who threw rocks; cars and state vehicles and construction trucks; the long gondola whirring when there was no wind. The buildings all year now shook with noise and lights. At night the windows dimmed and went silent. Here was the safest place and time to cross this ridge and perhaps the next ridge; to make a wide circle of other bears; to be alone; to move down across the forest, toward the streams, to fish and forage.

Katie put on her pack. Her ankle was swelling now; it would soon be stiff. They walked the trail single-file, cautiously, stepping carefully up and down the rocks, making little noise to announce their presence. So perhaps they surprised each other. The bear ambling toward them, doglike, taking its time, careful about the surrounding darkness. The hikers securing their footing and saying nothing in the last light. The bear must have seemed enormous: three and four times the size of bears at a zoo, outsized but also vibrant, so plain in its terror. The claws retracted. The snout closed.

How far away was it? Ten feet? Twenty? No one seemed to know. Katie's mind flashed options, calculating the intervening time and space. Three or four seconds. Did the bear *really* see them? Did the bear care that they were there? She thought, *We can run,* but she knew they could not outpace it. She thought to open the pack and find the pepper spray. Was there enough time? The pepper spray was zipped into a pouch inside the top pocket. If she dropped the pack and dug inside of it, then she might call attention to herself and distract the bear. It might charge. Of course, anything she did could provoke the bear. There was a space between them still; that was important. And maybe the bear had not yet seen them.

Katie was easily the most fit, the one who knew and loved nature. She looked to the two hikers behind her. How quickly did the surprise turn to terror? Was it in an instant? Was the understanding of their danger, and their mortality, obvious? Or, did they laugh at first? Were they shocked and overwhelmed? *A fucking bear!* Was that shock held in check by reason and optimism? There were three of them and only one bear. Could they, together, scare it off and escape the situation?

Katie looked at Sara, then the Romanian. No one did anything. They stood there, stock-still, and the bear approached.

How long had it been now? A few seconds? Katie took off her pack and threw it as far as she could in the other direction. Sara did the same thing. If the bear was hungry, it might follow the packs. The outer pouches were filled with candy, water, granola bars, dried fruit. They had only managed to toss the packs three or four feet, but it might give them enough time. They walked as a group, slowly and backward, shading just right, to open a distance between themselves, the bear, and the packs. If the bear followed, Katie told Sara, then it might still become distracted. It might break off its pursuit to find food. It might lose interest.

Did she imagine then they would all survive? Was she hopeful for it? The hill inclined toward the path, then the water. Bears were faster but perhaps not as sure-footed as humans. Could they make it to the rocks at the stream? Should they arm themselves with rocks and sticks? The pepper spray was in the pack, but perhaps with a few rocks and a little luck they could grab it.

Or perhaps this was the foolish option. The bear was large, heavy, resolute. It could charge at any moment. Why was Katie making these decisions? The bear continued forward, slow and deliberate. Katie said they should all play dead, so they rolled onto the ground and covered their heads. At what strange angles to the ground they must have held their bodies. How terrifying, that waiting in the dark for the attack to either begin or not begin, and thinking still, this might pass. They might survive all of this, if they only remained still and waited.

The bear pawed first at Sara and the Romanian, not Katie. It swiped at their heads, tore at their scalps and legs, pushed into their backs. They were injured and afraid but not yet hysterical. They continued to play dead.

They submitted to the bear, but the bear did not choose them.

Who was the first person to think of it? That one or two of them might survive if only one of them didn't? That they did not have to outrun the bear, or defeat it, or discourage it. Perhaps they thought of it like this: the odds are on someone's side. Individually, whoever ran first had only to get clear and back to the trail. If the bear did not follow, then it would be the other person who abandoned the victim. They had only to surrender the idea of the group, and wasn't the bear doing that already, focusing now on Katie, leaving them be? How long should they wait like that? Didn't each minute they stayed only increase the odds that the bear might turn back to them and take a second look?

Could they turn away from this last part of themselves? They did not have to want to do it. It could appear suddenly in their minds, a surprise, a well-reasoned and complete idea for which they had no agency. Fortune. Distraction. Survival.

Who worked out the math, the timing, the imperfect logistics, until running became the only real option? Who lay there, waiting to try it? How long did they wait? It seemed an eternity, this waiting, but it had only been a few minutes since they stood at the kilometer marker with the rest of the group, taking pictures. Hadn't the other group abandoned them there? The victims were here, while the survivors had gone ahead to the hostel to sleep for the night. Did anyone notice their absence? Hadn't they missed their window to catch up?

They must have heard a voice yelling Katie's name, then their own. Perhaps they recognized it. Should they respond to it? Did their voices risk unsettling the balance of disinterest and safety? Still, they were all alive. The bear seemed now more menacing than curious. It seemed to wait for something.

And then Katie's voice yelled back, sudden and louder than the wind on the ridge, clear and insistent.

Don't come closer. Find a gun. Get back quickly.

Katie had spoken. She had broken the silence.

The voice was gone now. A window of time was closing. Did any of them really believe that help would arrive in time? Now there was no longer obligation, only panic and its acceleration, and Katie, unable to move, laying stock-still on the ground, following the rules, still played dead and waited. She whispered to the others to leave, to go get help and come back. She watched them leave, and in the silence that followed, she understood she was now brave and selfless, heroic and elect, and that these were judgments that could come only after the fact of her death, in the witness of those who survived to speak of it.

I must tell this last part even if I do not know it. I have to think through how she made this decision and what happened afterward, even if I cannot know.

Katie lay on the ground, waiting. She made her body into a ball so that the bear could only strike obliquely. She covered her face and waited. She would not have felt optimistic or hopeful for herself, and she would not have felt good for the people she had rescued. Her mind did not work this way. There would be no pleasure, only a sense of obligation flashing once across her mind, to say she had done the right thing by the people she loved. She had saved them. Or, better still, she had given them the chance to save themselves. However they cowered from it and tried to refuse it, or say it was a matter of circumstance and timing and luck, always just below their complicated reasoning, their absence of guilt and refusal to explain, was the irrefutable fact of their witness. Katie had given them permission to leave. She asked them to do it.

In that moment, perhaps, Katie imagined her own death without consequence. She waited for it. Through the fear, the pain, and then the absence of pain. Long enough for her friends to get clear. Patient for what she knew now was the end. She heard the voices, closer, then further away. Then, no voices. No sound, no presence, no sense of self. Only the object of her body waiting to be received. Her mind becoming one part of that body, calling for help until it could not make words, only sounds, locating itself in the surrounding darkness. Then the mind, separate of that darkness.

It was roughly twenty minutes from the moment the two hikers left the hill until Katie's death, but in this last moment, she was not present. She could not be. The mind cannot organize so much pain and fear and suffering and also withstand it. This is the last, great lie of the surviving witness, and from everything I could find to read about trauma after Katie's death, it is also true. Katie's pupils opened to receive the last light coming across the ridge. She saw nothing. Not the stars or the grass or the bear, or the bear leaving and everyone arriving, slowly and too late, to claim her.

4. Sunday Morning

I stayed up the night with Katie's body. Local police, doctors, and reporters came through the room, performed or insinuated their duties, and left. It did not matter why they were there or when they would leave. I would never see them again.

Every half hour or so, I stepped out onto the hostel's porch to catch my breath. We had carried Katie's body about a quarter of a mile and laid it out on the basement floor. Someone thought to cover it with a tarp, which was pulled back with every arriving expert, who only confirmed the obvious. As though they had practiced it before, two or three people would stand me up and walk me to the other side of the room. I could listen to the various tests performed, but I did not have to watch them, a small grace for which I felt overwhelming relief and resentment. Who were they to deny me a place next to Katie? How could anyone think I would want to watch?

The place where Katie had died was only a few hundred yards away, but I couldn't see it. I imagined a sleuth of bears waiting there. I fantasized about killing them with my hands, braining them with large stones, spring-loading rusted traps that would stump their limbs and snouts. A bear would bleed out several days before it died somewhere, disoriented, alone, with only half a paw. Or maybe another bear would come along and kill it. Were bears hierarchical creatures? Empathic? I had no idea. The wind was blowing hard on the ridge. It was dark, cold and loud, and hard to listen or watch for anything from such a distance.

I was safe now, and I knew it. I would never put myself in harm's way again. I felt like a kid playing army with his friends in the yard.

However well I simulated the circumstances of Katie's death, I would never repeat them. Some part of me would understand it was a pantomime, just as I understood on the porch that I had had an opportunity to be truly brave, and I had failed. Or, I had stood as close to the danger as I could bear, but not close enough to make a difference. So, it wasn't like playing army; rather, it was like standing next to a large fire. There was a natural limit to the approach, which meant there was also a physical limit to my sense of the world. I had wanted to live. I had stood at a distance by a rock and watched my wife die. I had crouched in the neighbor's bushes, barely making a noise, trying to win the game by not getting caught, while my world burned around me.

No one seemed to notice my absence. We could do very little before morning. I signed forms and made decisions. I reported Katie's death in the careful detail that I had witnessed it. No one cared that I had not been heroic. No one asked me to explain my inability to protect Katie, my fear of her death, or the instinct to prevent my own. Didn't they know I had made futile gestures to intervene? That I had not really put myself in harm's way? This conversation kept not starting; that part of my answer kept getting lost or skipped over. I told the story again and again, slowing the night down, speeding it up, trying to keep the emphasis in the right places. The police distinguished motive from cause; if I had prevented Katie's death, then my actions would become part of the report. Instead, I was a witness. To them, the facts of her death, and my knowledge of them, exceeded my feelings of guilt.

The hunters understood why Katie had died. For them it was very simple. Katie was menstruating, and the bear smelled the blood. She was throwing rocks at a bear, and it charged her. We all had taunted the bear by taking photographs of it and next to it, testing its patience with us. We were Americans hiking on a mountaintop in the Buscegi Mountains on a late summer night. What did we think was going to happen?

The hunters moved to the far side of the room and set up a grill. There were sausages in the upstairs kitchen that someone brought down, then peppers and onions, then vodka and cigarettes. It was early in the night still, and no one would leave until morning. They spread out newspapers and sat eating their meals, smoking, and drinking. Much later the drinking would become a kind of carousing. The hunters laughed and played music on the radio. I hated them, and I could do nothing. This was their domain. I had asked for their help. Now, I was an intruder. My presence was a nuisance. When a reporter posing as a state investigator took video of me sitting in the corner, they stood next to me, asking questions so that it looked official.

The Israelis stayed up with me that night. The husband had a satellite phone. He said I should use it until the battery died. I called Katie's family, then my own, then the embassy. A friend of a friend took my call at the embassy help desk in Washington DC, and an hour or so later, the hunters received an official phone call, after which I was given a blanket and treated with excessive deference. The grill was closed, and with it their absurd intrusions were replaced with a solemn, post-Communist vigilance. Someone important was paying attention now. We waited in silence for doctors, then state detectives.

I had called Judy first and then promised to call her again. Here was another convenient form that my cowardice took. I stood in a basement on the side of a mountain in Romania. Just north of Chicago, Judy sat in a blue plush recliner by a digital telephone, waiting for my call. But I had nothing more to tell her. Or, I would know more when we left the mountain, but the situation would not change so long as we did not move. All day—my night—she waited. It was reasonable that I did not call again. Just out the living room window a neighbor had built a small fence to pen in the edge of her yard and keep the lines of the lawn narrow and clean.

I could apologize for Katie's death, but to whom could I explain it? In Chicago it was June, humid, sunny. I thought, *Katie has died in a place her mother will never visit.* A few days later Judy would call to tell me that she and Ed were flying to Romania. Could I take them to the mountain? But I did not want to go back there. Not that week and not a year later, when I called the airline and begged them to credit the price of my ticket to an account in my friend's name. What was I thinking, suggesting we go back? I knew what I was thinking. I thought that if I went back then I could be done with grief. I would transform the place of Katie's death into a memorial. I would dare the bears to come out and challenge me for it, and it would be daylight, and there would be tourists and hikers, and the absence of danger would mean Katie had been unlucky; there was nothing any of us could have done to stop her death.

Just before dawn two state officials arrived to oversee the end of our time on the mountain. There was a process to complete now and a corresponding solemnity. *Police Officers* became *Detectives. Doctors* became *Physicians.* For each step of the process someone gave instructions in broken English.

We will pull the sheet now back from Kathryn Evans's body, attach the heartbeat machine, and confirm no heart.

You are writing some sentences in the box to make record of the bear.

We wait just a few minutes. The ambulance arrives. We ride together.

As they prepared to move Katie, the sun came up. The sky, just blue, washed the morning in a terrific, pale light that made the hostel seem ramshackle, shrunken, its bright porch lantern one bulb hung over the porch. I turned to the ridge. I could see all of the way across it, to the second hostel. I thought, *I could cross in minutes and get back around the river without a hitch.* I could walk a circle around the place of Katie's death and make it sacred.

But then it was too late. We heard engines, and, coming up the slope, motorcycles and three-wheelers fanned out in a loose formation. In their red jackets and silly hats, I thought, they looked like Shriners. The theme from the *Benny Hill Show* looped in my head, but they got closer, and their manners were resolute and efficient, and when they stopped, Sara stepped from behind one of the machines and shook out her bright red hair.

I thought, *Her hair would still be that color if she had died.*

She was cold and tired. She walked with a limp. She had spent all night in the smaller hostel. Someone had given her two sleeping pills. As we approached each other, she smiled. She looked at me, but mostly over my shoulder.

There is a moment just after a trauma when the mechanisms of life become weightless. Everything that happens around you is solemn and professional, and it doesn't really matter whether you recognize how far the rituals and regulations of a culture range from basic necessities. Elaborate structures are put in place to support resolute and imperfect notions of continuity. You think, *The purpose of the living is not to understand or transform, but to survive and to make that survival incidental to the natural world and the individual life.* It is a balance but also a kind of trickery. In order to participate in the world, it must be tamed and made reasonable, and when it is not tame and reasonable, the world still requires participation. It cannot be witnessed. It is not transformed.

Of course, no one had told Sara that Katie was dead. They had left it to me. I should be the one to tell her, because she was my friend, and Katie was my wife. Or maybe no one had wanted to tell her or had yet seen the need. I didn't know that part, and I never would. She was the survivor. I was the widower. Katie's death was our common experience, but we would find no shared language to talk about it, no faith that would make it real and vital to each other, and close the gaps. Our experiences were singular, as were the stories we would tell about those experiences. Other people would listen and sympathize. And we would tell the story to other people.

A little over a year later, I stopped at the Lincoln Park Zoo and found the bear exhibit. It was closed for repairs. I was in Chicago visiting my siblings and had taken the afternoon to myself to visit the places Katie and I had loved. It was a good walk from Clark Street to the lakefront, then south along Lake Michigan. We had run this route when we were training for our year of half marathons and sprint triathlons, culminating in the Chicago Marathon that October, a week before Katie's birthday. Then, we were twenty-six. We had jobs and hopes for graduate studies the next year. We knew that we would leave Chicago, and we had no idea where we would go. But we liked to plan, so on those runs we mapped out logistics. What kind of city did we want to live in next? What sort of jobs and bosses, and where would we go after that? In the winters we would run the route I was walking now. We would strip off layers until we finished the loop in rubberized running shirts and sweat-pants, our hats, scarves, and jackets pushed into our pockets or tied around our waists. Steam rose off of our bodies, radiating some last heat against the wind and night. How vulnerable we must have looked, so rigged against the elements and seemingly out of place, walking at different paces, trying to catch our breath.

The bears at the zoo had been moved inside. It was humid, mid-summer. Probably, some part of me knew they wouldn't be out in such heat. I had imagined that if I looked at them and spent time near them, I might feel compassionate and brave. I would neutral-ize some part of my fear and, in so doing, change something about what had happened. Or, at least, what had happened to me. But I was a witness. My role wouldn't change. A small placard showed a photograph of two small black bears, each named for a local sports team, perched next to a tree only a few inches behind the plastic glass. Katie had been killed by a brown bear. I thought, *I can't even get the bears right.*

All of that happened much later. Before we left the mountain, the police searched the ridge and returned with our bags. They had recovered what they could from the torn packs. Sara and I sat together in the truck, and it followed the ridge, toward the city. We were going down the mountain now. One of us cried, then the other, but not together. Between long stretches of silence we looked at each other and out the window. We hugged. We smiled. We did not smile. What was there to say? We grieved without intention or consequence. The road was rocky and steep, the sun bright, the air crisp and clean. Periodically, we crossed a herd of animals or slowed down as the driver gently rolled one tire, then another over and across a boulder. Even accelerating through the flat parts, we made no better than ten, fifteen miles per hour. We drove for two and a half hours, downhill, with state vehicles, in daylight, until we reached the hospital in Busteni, where Sara was taken for an examination, while I waited for Katie's body in a room across the hall.

5. Departure

I left the mountain with Katie's body. I signed papers in Romania, and her body arrived eight days later at a morgue in Antioch, Illinois, Katie's hometown, where I stood on one side of the room while Judy touched Katie's hair and face. The skin was cold and soft, purple but not so changed that we could not look at the body. It was dressed in the outfit I had folded neatly into a plastic bag in Bucharest: blue shirt with small orange flowers and linen pants. There were shoes and socks, too. Her hands were tucked under a sheet.

We had agreed to arrive together at the funeral home. We would decide individually whether to go inside. It was a rare opportunity after Katie's death to make an individual choice and still be a part of the group. The funeral director walked from his office to the parking lot, into the muggy June heat, wearing a crisp blue suit and a dark red tie. Everything about his manner suggested kind reluctance. It was good, he said, that we had decided to come. He would mix lemonade for the children. When we were ready, we should walk into the small room with crimson wallpaper. There were prayer cards in the lobby. Katie's body was laid out on a metal table. The morgue opened from the door on the left.

We should know, he explained, that the body had not been prepared well for travel. It was not immediately cared for after the death. It had traveled a long way. Probably, we would not notice, but it was the sort of thing he looked for in his work. He would wait in the next room until we were done. We should take all of the time we needed.

I made myself stand near the wall with Katie's sister, and when Judy said it was okay to touch the body, I touched the body. I put my hands on Katie's forehead and tried to breathe slowly. The face was cleaner than I remembered. The skin had been washed and restored in places. Judy talked to Katie. We followed her example. I thought that I had said goodbye on the mountain, but here was Katie—her body—and a different group of people standing in a circle around her. Then, we seemed all to be praying. Why was that? I tried to think of good things to say or think. I muttered a few Hail Marys. I wanted to be reverent or to at least seem reverent, to participate and be supportive: a part of the group. But there was nothing new about Katie's body; it only looked different, I thought, cast in plastic. How had I let *this* happen? We had moved Katie's death to a new place and still it was not finished.

Already, friends, family members, and strangers were arriving in the room upstairs, to keep a vigil before the wake. We would speak, sing, and pray. We would stand at the front of the room, as a family, so that everyone could pay their respects. Tomorrow, on our way to the funeral mass, we would ride in the minivan. When we passed the fire station, the chief would turn on the sirens. It was a gesture of kindness and acknowledgment, this tribute, and I had not asked for it. I did not like it. The loud noise startled me. I felt rushed, conveyed to some hypothetical place past grief, a feeling, a forced memory. But we had not yet remembered the death. We had only just seen the body. It was Fourth of July weekend, and the day after the mass there would be a parade on this same street.

Before the mass we met at the funeral home to claim the ashes and say a prayer. The ashes were tied in a plastic bag snapped into a disposable tub that fit inside a lacquered wooden box we would return to the director the next morning. I carried the wooden box into the church. Katie's family followed. I thought, *Well, at least if I drop it, nothing will spill.* Once I stood in the pew, the service would begin. Once the service began it would end. I tried to imagine myself walking out of the church without crying.

During his homily the priest explained what a good person Katie had been. A loving daughter, sister, granddaughter, daughter-in-law, aunt, niece, and friend. The priest was recently retired. Judy had asked him to perform the service as a favor to the family. Before the homily I had had a sense of myself as the center of things. People were watching me, so I should act a certain way. I bowed my head and tried to keep very still. My mother sat behind me and periodically put her hand on my shoulder. I should be grateful for the large church filled with mourners, I thought, the ushers who had come as a favor to Katie's stepfather, the friends and family members who had traveled all that way to be there, my friends, my family, the firemen with their stupid siren, even the priest. I waited out the service, in full view, for everyone, and we walked yet again down the aisle, toward the light, and when we left the church, I took Katie's ashes with me.

We ate lunch on long benches in the church basement. Five or six picnic tables at the front, lined with hot plates donated by the wives' club. Baked potatoes with cheddar and bacon. Boiled green beans with bacon. Deep-fried bacon-flavored cheese curds. A vegetarian friend visiting from California asked if there was anything he could eat, and a volunteer suggested he try the iceberg wedge with ranch dressing. There were bacon bits in a bowl on the side. People were talking to each other now, scraping knives on plates, scooting their chairs across the linoleum. The luncheon was the end of the service, a built-in acknowledgment to the mourners, who had done something and would now return home and continue their days.

After the funeral we changed into shorts and t-shirts and met at a nearby county preserve. Ed and I had gone for a run together there earlier in the week and picked the place. We walked a mile out to a turn in the path where the preserve opened out. It faced a field filled with wildflowers. A smaller group, now, of family and good friends followed us. I had the ashes in the plastic bin in the tub in the box and a clear prewarning from the funeral director that what we were doing was expressly illegal, and we should return only the container that next morning. I liked him a great deal. Katie's uncle held the ashes, then passed them to someone else, and so on, until we arrived at the turn. We spoke still more prayers, some secular in nature this time, or perhaps they were not prayers but blessings. We spoke in turns, and when there was nothing more to say we opened the bag and walked out into the grasses and flowers.

The ashes fell in a single clump. The interior bag was heavy and caught at the latch of the container. People came forward to take turns scooping the ashes and scattering them. It became part of our ceremony. There were wildflower seeds that my mother had brought from a local florist. Later, Katie's mother and sister would confide that they had each put some ash in their pockets to take home, but at the time I imagined only that we had moved Katie to a new and final place. She would be welcome here, and she would have liked being so close to her mother.

The sun started to set as we walked out of the preserve. That fresh smell of damp, cut grass so particular to midwestern evenings came from all directions. Joggers passed us. We separated into groups. I held back a moment, thinking still that I would have something spontaneous to tell Katie; something clever and beautiful and poignant to say in her absence, when we were alone. Nothing. Two friends waited for me down the path, and we walked together, leaning into each other a while, quiet and relieved.

Where was it now, that sadness, the emptiness and isolation that had followed Katie's death, which terrified me still and had no name? Rather than transforming us, the day was ending. It could contain us no more certainly than Katie's ashes now waited to soak into the ground. A terrific thunderstorm started that afternoon and continued into the evening. Water filled the streets. Everything shined a few feet beyond our reach. Porch lights, billboards, flashing reds: all disappearing into the downpour.

That night, at the restaurant bar, I went back and forth between Katie's family in one room and my friends in the next. I felt that I should be present for Katie's family, to console, support, and grieve with them. I wanted to sit in a room with my friends and drink and sing sad songs. Hadn't I spent all day, all week, trying to honor some sense of obligation I could not name, which did not seem to end with Katie, marriage, sympathy, or judgment? Before the funeral I had wanted to be one kind of person after Katie's death: selfish or selfless, good or bad, earnest or cynical. Now, my own sense of need began, in the smallest way, to exceed what I could give to anyone. I was hungry with it.

A large group of Peace Corps volunteers came to Katie's funeral. They arrived, on a few days' notice, from everywhere, moving in a group, friendly with Katie's family, friends, and each other. I loved that they were there and that they knew Katie as someone particular, in a particular place, that had nothing to do with Antioch, Illinois. They filled the second room with a love, sympathy, nostalgia, and feeling that was entirely my own. Here was my tribe. I was so grateful for it.

As the night went on, I went less and less often into the first room. A friend brought out a guitar. Another passed a bottle of whiskey under the table—Katie's favorite, Johnnie Walker—as another friend poured from it into our soda glasses. We sang and cried, or I would sing and someone else would cry, as though we were taking turns, and though it wasn't happiness, it felt like happiness. Winnowing joy from the day. We ordered shots and beers and mixed drinks until we were snowed under. The room was emptying out, and it was last call. Most of Katie's family had left the restaurant hours earlier. Ed had stuck around, and we played a few songs, but we could not really follow each other. One of us was always leading and calling out the chords.

Then, it was time to go home. We stumbled into the parking lot and stood a moment by the car, saying goodbye to the Peace Corps group, most of whom disappeared down the street to the nearby hotel.

Man, Ed said, when we were alone. *Those people* really *liked Katie.*

I laughed.

Oh, Ed, I said, *she couldn't stand those people. They're here for me.*

Flush

1.

I received the balance of Katie's life insurance paid four times: spouse's death (accidental), spouse's death (abroad), dismemberment and death (bear), traumatic death (bear, spouse). It was enough money to settle the bills from the funeral, to cover the costs of settling into Indiana, and to buy a car. I would live for a year, support myself, and not work. I could grieve without distraction.

The need to grieve in concrete terms, with particular goals, had been made urgent by the regional embassy psychiatrist in Romania. We talked for two hours in Bucharest three days after Katie's death. His office was temporary and sparse, a windowless closet in the back room of the embassy basement. He worked there once, he explained, maybe twice a month. He had flown in on special assignment after the report of Katie's death, to meet me, to offer comfort, and to make an assessment.

Was I well enough to leave the country?

To whom might I pose a risk if I did?

He said all of this up front, with a friendly manner, insisting we should be very clear about our purposes that afternoon. His purposes as a psychiatrist and my purposes as both survivor and widower. The psychiatrist had a full beard and wore white sneakers. He spoke in the very general terms of consolation—*all right, now, nature, breathing*—even as his process must have followed a very particular method.

I told him my purposes were practical and narrow. I needed to travel with Katie's body back to Illinois. I wanted him to know that I was fine because the bear had not attacked me. I said that I did worry about Sara and the Romanian, but especially the Romanian, with whom no one had spoken since the attack. Did he get his rabies shots? Was he injured still? Could he afford a doctor? Someone needed to talk to him, to let him know that Sara and I were okay; we had survived and received medical attention. We had come down the mountain with Katie's body. I didn't want the Romanian to think that we had just disappeared or just left him there. That we weren't concerned for his well-being. We had had no choice that morning but to leave. There had been detectives; it was morning. We could probably get the Romanian the medical help he needed through our embassy, I explained, and that was important. Hadn't I already mentioned doing so several times to people at the embassy and Katie's office? I would call him myself, but there was no record of his last name or phone number.

I told the psychiatrist that I had stayed awake with Katie's body the whole night, and wasn't it a kind of accomplishment because who really does that anymore—hike all day, not sleep, and still function the next day—just as, really, it was no surprise that later, after we arrived in Bucharest, the embassy nurse had me over for a late lunch and to do a general physical examination. I had said that to her that I felt fine, even though I had not stayed up all night. Probably, when she examined me, I had seemed agitated and unsure of myself. I was tired. I had been running on adrenaline all day and night and day again, and while it was nice to talk with someone, I understood my purposes and needed to be on my way.

There was not a scratch on my body, I explained to the nurse, because the bear did not attack me. The bear had killed Katie. Sara and the Romanian had survived the attack, but I had stood at a distance.

At the nurse's house, I took a shower. I was starting to feel tired, and it seemed the right thing to do. Regroup. Refresh. Perk up a little. I stepped under the hot water, and immediately, though I was not certain, I thought that I heard, behind my head, in the next room a tick, a methodical clicking, like the tap inside a drain, a metallic whirring of a machine winding down: that was what it sounded like. When the click stopped, it made a silence in the bathroom I was terrified to interrupt. I stood under the water until I was sure I could move. I felt very still then. I counted my breaths and closed my eyes. I took a towel down and tried to scream into it, but instead I was sick. I leaned into the glass a moment, and when I turned off the water, I could hear people talking in the next room.

Wasn't I making this all up, I thought to myself; this feeling of uncertainty, this need for attention; this strange and clear center I was already claiming, from which I could not step away without worrying I would fall off the Earth?

I am fine now, I told the embassy psychiatrist, but I had sure had quite a shock. It helped to have pills from the nurse. She gave them to me after I got out of the shower, after I cleaned myself up and we talked. In the bathroom I had seen, through the mirror, my clothes in a pile on the bathroom floor. They were the only clothes I had with me, and after the shower I had to put them back on. It seemed stupid that I had gone to all of that trouble to shower, only to wear the same clothes again. The sleeves and pant legs were caked in mud. The t-shirt was rank and salted with sweat. My socks were stretched at the ankle and loose around the toe.

Sitting with me on the sofa, the nurse said I should take the pills if I felt overwhelmed or needed to sleep, but she wanted me to talk to the psychiatrist. I wanted to ask her, *How overwhelmed? How would I know when it was time to take the pills? What would it mean to need them?* I did not want to impose on her by asking too many questions; perhaps, if I did, she would wise up and not give me any medication. She might think I was using the occasion of Katie's death to score some grade-A pills, and then I'd really be stuck. No pills. No silence. No sleep.

The white pills, I told the psychiatrist, *worked at night like magic.* That morning I had taken two yellow pills, and the world now slowed enough so I could follow it. I could breathe. I didn't feel like myself, I said, but I didn't feel so afraid or confused as I had that night on the mountain, then in the car coming down the mountain, in the hospital with Sara, and later again at the nurse's home.

I was fine, I told the psychiatrist; my goals had to do with Katie. Her body. I needed to get Katie home to Judy. I needed to claim Katie's body from the undertaker and arrange for its transportation to Illinois before it went lost or missing. Judy should see Katie's body, and soon. I had heard a story about an American's body disappearing at the morgue and turning up years later in a museum, dressed in Soviet kitsch. I smiled at my joke, and then I felt great shame to be crying, in great heaves and sobs; I felt ashamed for making myself weak in front of this stranger and also disappointment that I was so unoriginal, unexceptional, and uncontrolled that I could not keep things together even for this meeting, this preliminary discussion, this test I needed to pass in order to leave Romania, to claim Katie's body and fly back home.

I feel safe with Katie is what I should have said.

If Katie were with me in the room, I should have told the nurse, then she would tell me what to do next. I wouldn't need to ask the embassy nurse for pills, or the embassy psychiatrist for help, or anyone why, since Katie's death, I had felt in such equal parts fear and excitement, even at night, as I fell asleep in a haze of narcosis and panic, uncertain how I might keep myself safe and protected for the seven hours I would not be conscious. *Katie kept me safe*, I thought, and though I knew this was sentimental, it was also true.

The embassy psychiatrist handed me a box of tissues and waited a moment. First, he said, my relationship with nature would be very different now. Something very similar had happened to him, and he had eventually come through, but it had taken time. It was not easy, but it was possible. Second, he said, probably I would not be all right for some time, if ever. And this was okay. I might recover enough to live, but I would never be the same person from a few days ago. I had been through quite a shock. My life would have *an integrity*—I remember this phrase exactly—but it wouldn't be the integrity I had taken up the mountain.

Third, he said, and this was very important, I should focus on leaving Bucharest as quickly and efficiently as possible. I should go to Katie's funeral, grieve with Katie's family and my own, and see my way to the end of the rite. Things would be easier for a while because there would be so much to do, but when things slowed down later, I should go see somebody. I should talk with a professional about what had happened. Above all I should do everything in my power to take care of myself. If I didn't, he warned, then I would not be all right.

2.

A few times it seemed likely I would not receive any life insurance payout after Katie's death. Katie had initially declined the policy, even though it was provided for free, as part of her work's benefits package. The paperwork, Katie said, was too extensive and exhausting to complete. She thought it was easier to ignore the form than to submit to the required physicals, blood tests, medical records, and statements of exemption. Now, her initial refusal was a red flag for fraud review on the claim. The situation of Katie's death was so extraordinary as to possibly warrant no coverage: *Act of God*, born of our poor judgment to hike into a mountain wilderness, across a well-known bear habitat. We had willed ourselves into a potentially fatal situation, the insurance agent explained. She handled this explanation so tactfully, and with such sympathy, that I did not really understand it until we were off the phone. A second agent that week called to clarify both the question and my answer. Had Katie and I, he asked, known we were hiking into a natural place where there were sure to be wild bears?

Thank you so much for your kind donation in Katie's memory to the Independence Center. It was a simple sentence. I wrote it seventy-four times on a cream card. I folded each card neatly inside an unsealed white envelope. I stuck a bright blue stamp in each corner. I thought of the route I had flown home from Romania, over the Antarctic: blue ice, white ocean. I remembered standing in security at Heathrow Airport, waiting for a tight connection, and screaming at the agent that I was accompanying my dead wife's body home and he should *let me into the fucking express lane to get on my fucking plane.*

Already I was aware saying such things might grant me certain advantages.

Two weeks after Katie's funeral, I sat at the kitchen table in Indiana. I was moved into the house now, and my bags were stored away. In front of me I managed a yellow legal pad filled with names and addresses. I called my parents and friends, and Katie's family, to coordinate acknowledgments. We were thanking everyone who had made a donation, in lieu of flowers, to the assisted-living facility where Katie's brother lived at the end of his life. Now, I had only to seal the envelopes and walk them to the post office.

The legal pad was ticked with finished and unfinished tasks. I called the bank and informed them of Katie's death. I requested that Katie's name be removed immediately from various accounts, that our joint credit cards be canceled, and that a new card be issued only in my name. Fraud after a death was common, the bank explained, and I should take a few simple steps to protect myself. I received in the mail an embossed folder outlining each step on heavy blue card-stock. The Social Security office processed its one-time payment; there was a more elaborate option, which might have yielded a larger payout, but I did not want to bother with it.

I contacted the State Department to request certificates of death in Katie's name. The certificates were notarized official copies, registered by the government. I gave them to former employers, banks, alma maters, insurance companies. Each time I altered some record of my continuing life by removing Katie from it. I ticked "Widowed" after "Married" and, where it did not apply, "Single." I made new piles of envelopes on the chair, with rolls of stamps and several pens.

From the insurance company I received all manner of warning about the vulnerability of widowed spouses, the ways in which even my own bank might prey on my bad judgment and guilt, the newspaper notices of deaths by which predators would pretend to have known Katie. The photographs on these brochures were of seniors, often women, sitting near windows in reclining chairs. I thought of the self-help aisle in the bookstore. The iconography of widowhood was again distinct and expressly excluded the young. Testimonials that consoled the death of a spouse—peace of mind, medical bills, inheritance claims—said little about the angst and worry of continuing to live for a very long time.

Would the insurance company make good on its check? Might someone steal the check en route? What if the check was mailed to the wrong John Evans?

I worried someone might contest the payment on the grounds that I had facilitated Katie's death in order to receive the paid benefit. No one could prove it, not really, but wouldn't there be a lawsuit, legal representation, courtrooms, judges?

Whatever money I received, I decided, I should give immediately to Katie's family. I was being compensated for Katie's death, so surely the compensation was not mine exclusively. Rather, it belonged to everyone. I would divide the check into portions and pay it out to each family member. I wouldn't say it outright, but they might infer that the money should in some way ease their sadness and so, perhaps, some of the obligation that followed after Katie's death. It might even work out to enough money that they would feel indirectly if genuinely pleased. It might make a difference in their lives, and they might feel some gratitude for the consideration. Who knew, it might even bind us together in the coming years: an obligation, an act of generosity so selfless we would have to love each other or at least keep in touch.

The check came in the mail six weeks after Katie's death, in quadruplicate, in a clear-windowed envelope, on a piece of perforated paper with a watermark. I received a sum of tax-free money greater than what Katie and I had earned together in the three years since we left Chicago. I deposited the check immediately, and a few days later it cleared. I was flush. As part of my daily ritual, I monitored the account, making a comprehensive record of every expense— grocery store, coffee shop, movie rental shop, and lunch out with the nieces—that drew it down. I calculated the interest of the savings account and wondered whether it might keep ahead of daily expenses and, if so, then for how long.

3.

The first night I arrived in Indiana, I came down with a terrific fever and cough. The neighbor, a family friend, came over with her doctor's bag, listened to my breathing, counted my pulse, asked me questions. I sat up in the bed, pulled the covers around my chest, and listened to her prognosis. I did not need to go to the emergency clinic, she explained, in three to five days I would feel better. The cough would subside. The congestion would loosen. Because my ears might fill with fluid, I should take a general antibiotic to prevent a broader infection of the lungs. The best thing to do was to get some rest. She wrote out three prescriptions: the antibiotic, a short-term prescription for antianxiety pills, and a long-term prescription for sleeping medication. Treating grief, she said, was like treating the symptoms of a patient with terminal cancer. I should take whatever I needed to get through the worst of it. As it got better, she explained, I could taper down the doses, in the regular care of a different doctor.

The morning the fever broke, I walked to the pharmacy in the strip mall and waited while my prescription was filled. The pharmacist said it would take twenty minutes. I wandered the aisles, filling my basket with every variety of remedy. Nasal sprays, antihistamines, cough suppressants, cough drops. Ear drops, ear plugs, wax removal kits, menthol rubs. Antacids, suppositories, hair-loss and shaving creams, antifungal pastes. Heavy and light syrups, flavored orange, bubble gum, strawberry, mixed berry, sugar free.

Which of them might cure anything?

Several bottles interchanged the same four or five ingredients mixed with sucrose and water, dried into powders and capsules. In the place of certain medications, a plastic card was fit onto a snap-away rack. These medications were so powerful I might transform them into poisons. The very mechanism of their distribution was mutable and, so, controlled. I might solicit them or make their chemicals unstable in laboratories, home bathrooms, high school playgrounds, my bloodstream. These drugs were not to be trusted to certain owners. They expired on a regular basis. Paperwork made accountable to state and federal drug agencies any desire to own them.

How far into the aisles might I wander before I inevitably turned back toward the pharmacist? Her office in the store was emblazoned with back-lit, neon letters three and four feet tall, outlined in bright plastic tubing, turned on in the morning and turned off first thing at night, before the store closed down, a regulated and regimented space from which all clarity might arrive, into which there would be no certain crossing, no means or way to step across the white badge, white jacket, white skin, and close-cropped hair, the white aisle behind which every drug and symptom, on white stacked shelves, waited to be summoned for the body's need, want, and desire.

I was accountable now. I was being watched. My driver's license was scanned; the number was printed on the bottom of the receipt, next to the legal percentage of each drug I might own in the remainder of the year. I signed one paper to claim my drugs. I signed another to agree I understood how to use them. At a booth, at the far end of the wall, a different pharmacist waited to make some explanations. A man stood behind me, with his own plastic cart.

Near the last aisle I sat down at a blood pressure machine. I unbuttoned and rolled up my shirt. I inserted my arm into the black cuff, all the way up. The machine clicked and whirred. The cuff tightened. The digital screen ran a circle of hashes. I waited for two numbers and checked them against the graph. For my height and weight, my blood pressure was high. Both numbers were outside of the normal range.

I walked back to the pharmacist and waited to ask my question. Did I need to worry about these numbers? The pharmacist explained that she was not a doctor. She could interpret and explain, but not evaluate. I should be sure to talk to my doctor if I had any concerns. The machine in the aisle, she explained, was only there to make approximate measurements. My doctor was the person to ask about my health, but could her colleague answer my questions about the drugs I was buying?

Was I doing something wrong? Was it right to ask the neighbor about the numbers? Should I report them to someone and hope for intervention, clarification, purpose, sensibility? A doctor would probably process the numbers into some system of accountability. Did I require supervision? Would I die soon? Did the numbers predict my death? Did they matter, at all? Or, had they already disappeared into the ether, never made certain; had they become nothing other than some red digital light shone briefly against my skin, reflected out under the fluorescent lights, bouncing back and forth against nothing, disappearing nowhere as the store's motion sensors recognized the movement of my leg, then opened the door to convey, even ferry me out of the strip mall and back to the world?

4.

From patterns of domesticity a persistent vein of illogic was made to shine. Nothing could ever be so singular as Katie's death. I grieved now to unsettle that initial caprice, to practice what I had learned on the mountaintop, that I should be ever vigilant of a world out to surprise and unsettle me. A world without mettle, overrun with collateral, kept the shadow of apprehension at bay and under the door. I had only to choose whether to resist or yield to it.

And yet, I had *money*. So much money I could only picture it in a briefcase, or a bank vault, or on a city street with banknotes fluttering comically in the wind. The money made me curiously welcome everywhere. It lost a small fraction of its value every day, then earned an even smaller fraction of its value back. I should spend it; the world seemed to be insisting I do so.

I worried I was an imposition, that I needed to counterbalance favor with acts of generosity. The line needed to zero out, so that the debt I incurred would not become too severe. The insurance check had a serial number, zeroes, a line of endorsement, my name in embossed letters, and two or three markers to guard against duplication. It expressed a precise figure that was not negotiable, blackened in block letters across the middle, squared by edges embossed with gold and green finish. All I was required to do to relinquish the amount was to accept it, then slowly give it back to the world. An accountant said I had no financial reason to give the money away to Katie's family. My sister-in-law said no one had any expectation that I would suddenly give away money, and the less Katie's family knew about it, the better. It might only further complicate a raw and volatile dynamic. My sister suggested I put the money away for a while, that I make two portions: enough to live on for the moment and the rest to save for later. Everyone, she said, always needs more money. It is good to save, the therapist agreed, a continuing life requires it.

I made the decision quickly: in a few days. I thought, *This is just how it happened on the mountain. In a moment of true self-evidence I am not a generous person. Or, I want to be generous, but I cannot act on the intention. I cannot suffer the risk. Instead, I protect myself.*

I received sympathy cards, letters, and still more notices of donations made in Katie's name, phone calls. Friends who annotated them with memories and condolences posted photographs of Katie on the blog. It was a simple and beautiful time that did not hurry and would not last. I was prodigal and humbled. On an especially busy afternoon I walked to the strip mall, shopped for clothes or toiletries, and then walked back home. Every few weeks I drove to the mall and bought inexpensive trinkets and elaborate gadgets. I paid rent, mailed gifts to Katie's family, and did my best to pick up checks at family dinners. It gave me pleasure to spend the insurance money, thinking about Katie as I bought bakery bread, organic milk, imported chocolates, microbrews.

I filled out forms connected to the new account. I called Katie's family and said I would like to give their information to the bank in order to make them beneficiaries. I wrote out social security numbers, addresses, and dates of birth. Katie's family would receive the balance of whatever was left after my death. Whenever I checked the balance now, I saw beneath it four names: Ed, Judy, Katie's sister, Katie's father. I felt both generous and stingy. I no more expected to die in Indiana than I had in the apartment in Bucharest, when Katie and I had signed the insurance contract. And yet, then as now, I asked for the consideration. That my presence in Indiana, and around Katie's family, was genuinely appreciated, even welcomed, seemed as remote a possibility as Katie and I ever choosing to live again in the Heartland. I acknowledged that, in the event of any such future catastrophe, I would need money, and so, they might, too.

The local notary received her business at the nearby Kinko's. We sat across from each other at a plastic table, and in plain language we discussed the financial obligations of designating Katie's family on the account. The process was formal and exact. She read out loud each line, then I signed, and then she countersigned. At the very end she pressed her seal into the paper so that it made its indentation and shape.

I appreciated her help, I told her. I was eager to be done with the process. How many times a day did she notarize documents? I was her first client that afternoon. The designees are my wife's family, I explained, but she's dead now. She died a few weeks earlier in Romania, where we had lived for a year. She was killed by a bear and I had been there. I had seen it happen. I was only now living in Indiana for a short while, with her family—with her brother's family, who lived down the street—until I understood what I should do next, and in the meantime I needed to notarize these beneficiary forms, then send them to the bank with the certified copies of Katie's death certificate, so that, if I died, Katie's family would receive some of Katie's money and maybe appreciate having it and also think well of me.

The notary said nothing right away. Later I was grateful for her discretion. I immediately felt ashamed for saying so much to a stranger, even as I understood I was doing this sort of thing more and more often. I was telling people I did not know about the great recent tragedy of my life. Why was that? If it was a pattern, then I might be a manipulative and opportunistic hustler, seeking minor advantages. If it was an exceptional reaction, even a spontaneous one, then I might be the designated mourner, carrying forward Katie's life after its end. Probably, I was in shock, grieving, irrational. There was a place for the absence of sense; strangers recognized and accommodated it. The notary and I sat together a while, and I thought for a moment we might hold hands or cry together. Instead, she closed her stamp, and when I went to pay her, she refused the fee, wished me well, and said she would keep both my wife and me in her thoughts.

From what table of calamities and misfortune did two axes on an actuarial table resolve at the moment of Katie's death? Who decided its financial value? Age, work experience, circumstance of death. Nationality, gender, surviving family, health. In graduate school, for a small fee, Katie and I had participated in a biometric calculation of our respective longevities, based on weight, strength, flexibility, and aerobic capacity. Katie's *body age* was judged thirteen years younger than her physical age. Calamity was an unlikely probability, as it was in Bucharest. The insurance policy was a minor benefit of employment. Would someone else now pay a fee so that my receiving the payment increased the premium of some ex-pat living in Eastern Europe, for another fifty, eighty, one hundred years? A friend from the Peace Corps had lost his hearing in Bangladesh—infection, nerve damage—and received a few months later a check from the government, with a short letter containing the table of amputations and lost functions from which different amounts were determined. Had it been his hand or foot, he would have received three times as much money.

A process for surviving calamity was standardized, even monetized, so as to be inclusive and accommodate any largesse. That process required the beneficiary to feel placated and the payer to remain solvent. Did I submit to this system by accepting Katie's life insurance? Or was it something less generous to be paid off to stay for a while in one place; to receive counseling and medication as a protection to society; to keep a secret about nature and the world from which Katie had been removed, when no amount of money could restore her presence? What part of me felt happy to be acknowledged by that process? To be relieved of my own anxieties about wellness? Didn't Sara and the Romanian deserve to be compensated, at least as well as I had been, if not more so? The sum was so large that I felt as if I owned something alongside my grief, which might initiate some sense of obligation for my own vitality. The process required a different kind of order.

Katie was a number now, a fact of place, a consequence in a life. Nowhere did it say her death was witnessed. Only that the body was observed, officially, many days later, and determined to be dead. And many days after that a generous sum of money to which no one else could make claim was entirely my own. A gift. A fortunate coincidence. The order of a world, seemingly restored. A minor, unassigned deception, practiced in Katie's absence, which I quietly deposited into a bank account, so that my life might continue.

The Number Line

Two days before Thanksgiving, I drove thirteen hours to a resort in Newport, Virginia, to spend the week with my family. We had not all been together since Katie's funeral that previous July. My parents' home, so near the North Miami campus where Katie and I had lived for the better part of three years, spooked me enough to avoid it. For our first holiday without her, we would meet on what my sister-in-law jokingly called *neutral ground*.

Our rented apartments looked out onto golf courses. Bright fairways and roughs shot improbable swaths of color into the late-autumn darkness. We spent our time at swimming pools, sitting in spas, eating second plates at buffets filled with lunch and dinner. We watched rented movies, played board games in antique shops, and walked across the nearby William and Mary campus. I was sad, and I missed Katie. But I was also relieved to be somewhere new, with my own family, practicing, at least for this short trip, older routines and dynamics.

A sense of two realities—grief and widowhood, there and here—was new. I wasn't sure what to do with it. In Virginia my family cared for me. They wanted me to get better. They hoped I might continue at least some part of a life interrupted by Katie's death. There was a welcome lightness in how we spent time together, a corny mix of humor and sentiment that persevered, even when it was willed. We wanted, more than anything, to have a nice time together. My father made thoughtful toasts about Katie before our dinners. My mother put out a booklet of photographs on a glass table. She kept a citrus candle lit in front of it whenever we left the apartment.

Our last night in Virginia, after nightcaps and dessert, we followed signs to "live music," a local band playing country and rock covers in a small room just off the eighteenth hole. We ordered sambucas, then whiskeys, and made toasts to Katie. My sister got it into our heads that the band should play songs that Katie liked. We folded ten- and twenty- dollar bills into cocktail napkins and sent requests for Willie Nelson, John Prine, Lucinda Williams. We struck up a bit of a rapport. When the guitarist said he didn't know the words to "Sweet Caroline," I stood at the bar microphone, sweat soaking through my shirt. I laughed, cajoled, and performed, more than a little self-conscious. My family danced. A few tourists laughed and cheered.

What kind of a widower, I thought, *sings Neil Diamond with the bar band five months after his wife's death?*

Where was my sense of decorum and obligation? The band and tourists did not expect it. My grief, in fact, had nothing to do with their good time. It did not seem at all unusual that I stumbled back to the table, ordered another drink, and ate some peanuts. I suppose it wasn't. After last call my sister-in-law took some bottles of wine to go. Back at the room we were exhausted. We fell asleep watching movies.

The next morning I drove back to Indiana. Ten days later I got into the car and drove east, to New York City, then to central New Hampshire, to visit a friend. I wanted to be surrounded for a while by people I did not know very well, in a place I had never been before: not with Katie, or her family, or my family, and certainly not by myself. I spent the holiday in a large house in the woods. I loved it there. I was on the side of a mountain, in a warm, glassed-in room surrounded by trees and snow. On Christmas morning, when I came out of my room, everyone had already gone off to ski down the nearby pass.

After Katie's death I wasn't sure how to balance competing senses of obligation to family. I wanted to disappear into one family. I wanted to comfort the other. I knew that one family was permanent; I would always be a son and a brother. I might have only so long still to be a brother-in-law, son-in-law, cousin-in-law, uncle. Perhaps this was an unfair imposition into both families, one that made simple gestures of support reciprocal and binding. It was easy to believe there was nothing more important in the world than Katie's death, whether she was sister or sister-in-law, daughter or daughter-in-law. To me, in the beginning, the roles were equivalent. Certainly no one seemed to dispute it. Still, I came to fear that someone, somewhere, was keeping an account. A bottom line in a record would indicate an amount to settle for choosing one side. I might pay into the debt, or pay down interest on it, and keep ahead of it a little, but eventually it would come due.

Or perhaps it was better to think of the two families as a number line, with me as zero, stretching in opposite directions, all the way to death, end points that simply fell off the grid. I needed to define segments. I wanted to believe that the whole piece had direction. Perhaps I was exempt to the basic, algebraic logic; in Katie's absence the integrity of the line might not hold. Or, it was not a line but instead a pile of dominoes set on a track. Once they began to fall, there would be acceleration, collapse, and finally silence.

I picked up Ben at Kennedy Airport a few days after Christmas. He had flown from Berkeley to make the trip with me back to Indiana. There was just enough time that afternoon to visit the house in the city where I had lived alone with my parents during high school. Then, the house had seemed outsized and ancient to my transplanted Kansan eyes; dim, stuffy, and guilty of that cardinal sin of midwestern suburbia, that it was not, and did not seem to want to look, *new*. Now, I could only remember loving that house for its oddities and nooks. The miniature bathroom under the staircase. A long attic stuck up in trees. A flat side of the roof out which I could climb to sneak cigarettes. It was our home in Kansas that was less certain in my memory: summer-evening games of tag, bike rides, church picnics.

We drove into Pennsylvania, talking about Katie, therapy, Ed and Beth and the kids, movies, bands, books we were reading, my teaching, his work as a journalist. At the Somerset Diner a waitress gave us directions to the Shanksville Memorial site. The entrance was a few miles off the road, behind an unlocked gate, over a hill backlit by the city. Rain, then snow melted on the windshield. For ten minutes we ran the heater on high, idling while two deer never quite crossed our high beams.

I wrote Katie's name on the back of the diner receipt. I would leave it at the memorial. But when I stood, finally, at the long V of names taped with flowers under the plastic, written across pictures and photographs, or co-opted into typed statements of vengeance and retribution about terror, violence, and the government, the makeshift cement wall seemed suddenly too accommodating, as though it might not return whatever was offered it. We could only make our impromptu pilgrimage there, to wail, gnash our teeth, and curse the heavens, so long as we left something. The accumulation and momentum of many deaths made the place sacred.

Wasn't this what I was trying to tell Ben about Bucharest: that Katie had liked it so much because it made her feel both anonymous and distinct? "Romanian Gigolos: First Night Free." It was a fashion that summer. Throughout Bucharest, embossed in gold letters on green fabric, the phrase stretched across the chests of skinny boys walking in groups or smoking cigarettes with their girl-friends in the park. Katie loved the gawky chic, the sweet undertones of irony, the toothless sexism; how, out of habit, walking in front of a basilica, the kids would always pause to silently cross themselves. Katie kept meaning to get to the market to buy the shirts for friends, but then the fashion passed, or whatever stock of cheap cotton tees finally ran out, and finally it was only the idea of a gift, one she had kept for herself. Maybe, she said, she would find a press online to print the shirts and mail them back home. Eventually, the garish neon poked up only occasionally under the open collars of long-sleeved shirts or on a lone chest somewhere else in the city, utilitarian, warm against the skin of people we did not know.

I wanted to tell Ben that the first part of grief had seemed very simple—mourn, withstand, survive—while this next part required diligence, speed, a specific plan and intention. With whom could I still mourn Katie's absence in my life? Where would the emphasis settle each time I tried? I had carried grief at first so that everyone would see it, maybe even be forced to acknowledge it. Now I had to learn how to step back and protect it, to cover my body and reveal only what I needed someone else to see. In a lesser moment I thought, *I am Superman learning to become Clark Kent; I have a double identity and a corresponding, exceptional weakness to hide from everyone.*

I was beginning to make choices I did not quite understand. Katie's death was my story to tell, yes. Because I had seen her die, I was the witness to her death, and I could choose to tell that story. But I had also been unable to prevent her death. And this meant making a far more complicated distinction. Either I decided the bear had been large, terrifying, and impossible to head off that night, which meant that anyone might have survived or died on the mountain. Or I decided that I could in fact have saved Katie's life and simply had chosen not to do so. If I chose the former, then my witness was the inevitable fact of Katie's death. It might as well be a story told by someone else. Then I could surrender my guilt at not being able to save Katie because there was nothing to do. But if I chose the latter, if Katie could in fact have been saved and I didn't save her, if the bear would, in fact, have been attacked, distracted, or discouraged, at least enough that she survived, then I might have died, too. I was the only person who could tell that story: my failure. Week after week this was the distinction I could not tease out with my therapist. Had I been the witness or the coward? Driving with Ben, talking it out over and over, the distinction refused to settle.

My siblings arrived in Bucharest after Katie's death to help with my departure. We spent a week making lists, contacting officials, closing down the apartment, shipping cats. We attended together two memorial services for Katie, a public service at a basilica, and a smaller service in her work office. Katie's officemates had decorated her desk with photographs and candles. We drank brandy, pouring out onto the carpet a first sip for Katie. For the rest of our time in Bucharest, then back in Illinois, we repeated the custom.

There were so many details to the relocation of Katie's body. Insurance claims, embassy paperwork, long-distance shipping, meetings with Katie's former boss to decide the language for the international press release, the ambassador's condolence, the patriarchate's official statement. We were exhausted and overwhelmed, and yet we knew that, upon arrival in Illinois, it would all continue. The wake and funeral, explaining everything to Katie's family, greeting and thanking other mourners, the spreading of ashes, public and private dinners, hotel bills, conversations about and tributes to Katie. I believed, and said at the time, that my siblings' actions were heroic, but I also felt anxious for what lay ahead. Who could I lean on next? Who would help me get through the coming days and weeks?

In our hotel room, at night, I wrote email updates, reached out to friends on Skype, and talked constantly to Katie's family. The rest of the time I tried to manage a delicate and forthright silence.

As we spread Katie's ashes, Judy and Katie's sister each took handfuls into their pockets. They did it to prevent the end of the rite, perhaps, or to keep a part of Katie for themselves. Maybe they were addled by grief and vulnerable to its excesses. I believed this for weeks, until I decided, after talking it out with a friend, to take the much simpler view. I had no idea what they were thinking or why anyone did what they did. But I wanted Judy to be happy. I wanted to protect Katie and to keep sacred her death ceremony and our invented rite. The body I had taken such care to convey down a mountain, into a city, across an ocean, through customs, and finally to the small town in northern Illinois that Katie had spent her whole life avoiding would never be whole or wholly in one place again.

I agreed with Katie's family about so many things: collages of photographs for Katie's wake, hymns and passages chosen for services, how to stand together and thank people for their sympathy and generosity. We thanked the funeral director for his discretion and asked him to convey Katie back to us for our final, private rites, which we practiced together. We loved Katie for many of the same qualities and reasons. We spoke with great feeling about her absence, our memories together, and what she might yet have done with and away from us.

We accommodated together our need. I resisted those parts of a spectacle that had nothing to do with Katie and everything to do with the intersections of grief and minor celebrity: radio interviews, obituaries in local free newspapers, the order of eulogists at the mass. I had the legal rights of a husband. I was final arbiter. *Katie's sister, brother, mother, and father will speak*, I explained to Katie's stepfather. *You know, the family.*

After the insurance check cleared, I plotted an elaborate expression of my gratitude to my brother and sister. I hired a babysitter for the kids and paid for my sister's plane ticket from New York. I made reservations at a restaurant that I knew my brother liked. That evening a horse-drawn carriage arrived at their courtyard and ferried us to the Loop. Well south of my old apartment in Uptown, plodding down La Salle, the city was still bright with the end of summer. Streetlights came up over full trees. Cars made the rush hour commute in the opposite direction. Our relative progress seemed so earnest, methodical; we slowed at stoplights, waiting to follow the traffic. At the restaurant a bottle of chilled champagne waited in a bucket next to the table. We drank bottles of wine and picked over plates filled with meat, cheese, and pasta. As dessert arrived, I made a toast. I had practiced it, but not so much that the feeling was not genuine. Was I trying to settle the account, to pay off my siblings for their earlier generosity? Were my siblings honored guests, or was I asking them again to do something extraordinary: to receive my thanks but also to witness again my grief? *Gratitude is merely the secret hope of further favors.* I had read that somewhere. Between courses I made my way to the bathroom, where I locked the stall door, slouched into a corner, and tried to catch my breath. I felt the pressure ease a little. I washed my face, blew my nose, and returned to the party.

Every few weeks I showed up at my brother's apartment and spent the weekend at the park, going to the sandwich shop with my nephews, watching the Cubs on WGN. Some nights he and my sister-in-law would go out, and I would stay in and not do much; or my brother and I would go to a nearby bar, and my sister-in-law would watch the kids; or my brother would be traveling for work and my sister-in-law had night classes, so I watched television with the babysitter. In our old city, I visited old friends. It was a two-mile bus ride from my brother's neighborhood to the neighborhood where Katie and I had lived for three years. I watched a man in a blue jumpsuit, bobbing his chin under headphones, polish off a five-pound bag of pretzel M&M's between the eight stops.

It was beautiful to leave the home in Indiana where I lived with Katie's brother and his family every few weeks. I understood that, however life continued in one place, it continued also in another. Where did this neutral ground end? I arrived in Chicago on a Thursday and was taken in, fed, sheltered, and given a quiet place to read, sleep, and grieve. I left the following Monday, as everyone set off on their week's routines, and most of the time I felt refreshed and restored, emergent from a very specific withdrawal. Then I would arrive back in Indiana to a place where I was again taken in, fed, sheltered, and given still more solitude and space.

At the North Street underpass for I-94, I could take the onramp east toward Indiana or west toward Katie's hometown. The highway continued in both directions, but I couldn't see where I would ever really get clear. Iowa or Ohio. The Rockies or the Appalachians. Two oceans, then two continents where Katie and I had lived for a time, and finally the central point toward which everything seemed to converge—Istanbul maybe, where we had spent my twenty-ninth birthday together, or St. Petersburg, where we had always meant to travel—before the journeys turned in opposite directions.

Time and again, with the same few people, I told the same few stories. Themes emerged, then repeated: failure, good intentions, absence, limitation. I defended myself from certain accusations. I anticipated, even preempted criticisms. Always, in this defense, I was desperate in my failure. I had done all I could to save Katie. Night after night, I wrote down in a journal the story of her death without looking at the previous entries, then crosschecked them across different days. I needed to audit the public version of my story against the private, the told story against the true one. But it was the secondary narrative of my survival that people were most interested to hear. How was I getting better? How did I live now?

Details came forward with more than a little polish. Katie's sense of charity, her big-heartedness toward family, her willingness to mentor and advise. *Saint Katie*, as Beth joked we might remember her. We knew better. It was easier to imagine this version of Katie—the martyr, the cipher—just as it is was convenient to bring forward myself, and the things I wanted after her death, now, as a kind of contrast. *Charitable John. John the Beneficent. Saint Johnny.*

My confessions prompted exchanges. Sometimes, the sharing became reciprocal. People said things about themselves and how they made sense of the world after their own tragedies: pills, doctors, deaths, secrets. What was the limit of such empathy? I had never felt so close to so many people. I learned and shared things I never expected to know. The cost of such honesty and transgression seemed, at best, uncertain. It was one thing to comfort a grieving widower with secret knowledge, believing all the while that the listener was pathetic and feeble. It was another to crash in the boundaries that had shaped years of interaction, familial and otherwise. It was possible that we might grow closer, now, and more honest as a result. But perhaps later, we would need new boundaries and discretions.

I met my friend Stephanie at a bar in Kankakee, Illinois, three weeks after I moved to Indiana. She was in town for a conference the next day, so we met at her hotel, then spent all afternoon at a local brewpub overlooking the river, just past the small downtown. Until that morning I was not entirely sure I would make the two-hour drive. It was just close enough to seem a great distance to travel and return in a single night. But what else did I really have to do? I printed directions, plugged in my music, and set off.

We drank beer all afternoon. We ate chicken wings and garlic fries. We walked down to the river and sat on stone benches, counting sailboats and talking about Katie. I said I was scared I had not yet felt the worst of it. Wasn't more fear always just below the surface; wouldn't it come forward as the immediate grief rites ended, and the long slog of whatever happened next began? It was easy and calming to talk it all out; even when I turned the conversation to Stephanie's wife and family, she brushed off the pleasantry and turned it right back to me. I could do anything, she kept telling me. I had a brief window when no one would hold me accountable, when I would be given a very, very long piece of the rope.

Stephanie's stepsister had been widowed a few years earlier, also violently and suddenly, and had not taken care of herself after the loss. A quick and positive resilience to grief and mourning after her husband's death was sustained, increasingly, with narcotics, speed, poor decisions, distraction, recklessness. Everyone agreed that in the beginning she was so brave. Then she moved near the ocean, took up with another man, and they blew through the insurance money in weeks. When she finally broke, it was spectacular and final. She worked small jobs now and did not take on too much. She had children with two other men and abandoned both of them to her parents. She was in some ways her former self, but mostly she was an empty space, a cautionary tale about how not to grieve, a rock in a river around which the world, her family, and friends navigated, continuing their lives with great care.

Stephanie spoke in the reasonable, authoritative tones of a witness. I trusted her, and so I believed it was important to trust the precedent. Stephanie wanted to take care of me, but she also understood the limits of empathy. The world, she said, was presenting me with two very clear and unfortunate options. Withstand, and so move forward with some aspect of a new life unrelated to Katie. Or, retreat into my former life, and sacrifice the rest of it to Katie's death. Whichever I picked, I would not easily walk it back in the other direction.

We sat a while longer, talking about our lives in Miami those three years, Saint Katie, the deep well of grief that seemed only to rise and crest when I was angry about something else. And then it was time to head back to the hotel and say goodbye. The gas station just off the highway had a chintzy display of overpriced, Christian-themed trucker wear: t-shirts and handkerchiefs, vests and mud flaps and mirror guards. Stephanie picked a pink corduroy ball cap with rhinestones ornamenting the phrase, *Jesus, Take the Wheel!* Because Jesus can't drive, she said, laughing. She insisted I wear it on my drive back to Indiana.

When she was alive, Katie and I drove everywhere together. Always, we started in one place and arrived, quickly and efficiently, in the next. Now I wondered: how long could I stay in a car, on the highway, before I really needed to arrive anywhere?

I-65 was one of seven highways that ran spokelike from Indianapolis out across the state. I could return to the city, circle it, and go anywhere else. Why then was I always choosing Chicago, resting a while then leaving, bouncing quickly between two families like a nervous pinball? I told myself I was looking for Katie, but I knew that wasn't true. She was gone now, and life continued everywhere without her. I said I was retracing a memory and making sense of a loss. But I had at best a cursory knowledge of our few days together. I had not known Katie would die. I recorded the particulars of the world around me now in painstaking detail, but they did not seem to add up to an especially compelling sequence or sense of order. It was all marked time, meant to fill this gap between when I was broken and whenever I emerged, finally, healed.

Jesus, Take the Wheel! I worked the brim until it gave at the edges. I pulled it down low across my eyes. Life was so slow now. I had spent all day with Stephanie, and it was only six o'clock. I had been back in the United States a little more than a month, and it was only the end of July. I lived a year in Indianapolis. Before I left, I would turn thirty-one. Everything I said that first summer seemed to express its half-life in minutes, seconds. Numbness, irritation, anger, shock: these feelings were to the listener mere symptoms of a deep and abiding grief I could never really understand, which would one day pass. I seemed in terrible shape, and it meant that I had been through something awful but also that I had really, truly loved Katie. They knew it. Or I merely convinced them of something they wanted to believe. In the end what did it really matter?

I had forgotten the emptiness inside of cars on long drives, the way loud music can fill them and bounce off the glass, the easy and quick way a wheel slides a car across lanes. Alone, I could play the same songs again and again; singing at the top of my lungs, crying, screaming, and making still no explanation for the intervening silences. To drive, then, to be in a car pointed in a direction, gave me the thing I missed most in life: intention. This was my Fortress of Solitude, exactly between two places, neither arriving nor departing. And yet, I drove fast. I tried to keep to the schedule I had given Katie's brother before I left that morning. How pathetic and uncertain I must have looked, a large man in a tiny car, racing down the highway, the same few Bruce Springsteen songs always shaking the frame. How small I felt. It didn't really matter when I arrived back at the house. No one was waiting for me at a particular hour. No one was following close behind or eagerly tracking my progress. At whichever moment I finally pulled up the drive, Ed's family would already be asleep or long since gone off to bed.

The Circle Game

The goal was to get better. The method was talk therapy. The premise was that it was not my fault that Katie had died, so I needed to find a better explanation for both the tragedy and the interruption of my life.

We used this word constantly: process. Therapy was a process. Survival and witness were processes. Marriage and family were a single process teased elaborately into infinite, abstract, and repeating parts. It seemed that an entire life had conspired to make me garrulous and uncertain at precisely the moment I needed to talk. I could explain and rationalize, but I did not really understand. How had Katie and I ended up on that particular mountaintop, at that time of year, in that part of the world? Why the Buscegi Mountains of Romania and not, say, the Adirondacks or Rockies? The Himalaya? Why didn't we take the train further west and north toward Hungary or Iasi, to a festival or metropolis rather than the blank natural landscape of central Romania?

The scope of other questions seemed less certain after Katie's death. What part of me resented finding Katie that night on the mountain? Which part followed her blindly all day and hoped for the best? How far in any direction should I pursue an argument for or against myself, before speculation, rather than sense, became the guiding ethos? What did it mean to speak honestly and directly about Katie to a therapist? To Katie's family? How much would I need to describe to get better? Which parts did I want to leave out?

The therapist I met with in Indiana wore turquoise jewelry and smiled when she was not talking. She had a way of looking both at and through me, and it did not feel unpracticed. She counseled only trauma victims, and her office resembled an outsized children's playroom: board games and rag dolls, a desk in one corner, two overstuffed chairs, and a butterscotch dish between them on a Plexiglas table. She had been doing this for twenty-six years, she explained, and people from every walk of life had come through her door. Firemen, police officers, soldiers, teachers, business executives, families, and college dropouts. The tone of our conversations was friendly and reassuring but also forthright. The process would only work, she explained, if I followed it carefully and diligently, two and three times a week at first. We would name the problem, face it, make a context for it, and eventually I would learn to live with it. Like everyone else.

If there seemed some predetermination in her method, then it also excluded more extreme and prescriptive methods. There would be no antidepressants and mood stabilizers. I would not drink or smoke. I would get a job—any job—quickly, and I would not miss work to grieve. I would not seek out a support group or attend group therapy; my situation was exceptional, the therapist explained, and any group situation would only magnify the singular experience of Katie's death and lead to resentment. I would sleep, every night. We would keep an appointment every Tuesday, Wednesday, and Saturday morning at 7:00 a.m. I would arrive ten minutes early and pay her fee in full before I walked out the door on the hour.

Talking felt good. I left our sessions feeling relieved of a burden I could not yet name, and even as the burden returned, between sessions, I was certain I could keep ahead of it. In therapy I tried to share everything, even overshare. I believed no piece was so exceptional I should exclude it from the consideration of Katie's death. Whatever I said or thought to say was probably connected. It was all a rich tapestry, though this last part was my own ironic commentary, a tone that was not especially clarifying. I found more straightforward tones.

My first week in Indiana, I tried two other therapists. The first ran a practice in the basement of a church; our meeting was brief. The second had just opened a new, expanded practice, to complement the more traditional work she had done previously with clients. She was a life coach who, she explained, healed the brains of trauma victims with lasers. This involved shining a pen light at the wall, then into my eyes, until we located and rewired the physical part of my brain that stored trauma. After only a few sessions, she told me, I would begin to notice definite results. Fewer night terrors, waking dreams, and flashbacks. A greater feeling of peace and serenity.

I had read about the practice online. Eye movement desensitization and reprocessing showed great promise for victims and survivors of trauma, especially soldiers returning from Iraq and Afghanistan. Insurance companies were beginning to cover it and sometimes recommend it in lieu of talk therapy. There was much research to indicate that, in fact, the brain did store traumas in places the pen light reached; the brain could be healed without the anecdotal complications of storytelling.

At our only session the therapist dimmed the lights and flashed the red dot on the wall. She touched my knee and told me to relax. Everything would be fine. If I wanted her to stop at any time, I should just say so.

As she started the countdown and initiated the process, I could not stop staring at the business card holder on her desk. It glowed in the dark. I thought, *How can someone with a glow-in-the-dark business card holder heal me?* I felt bad for her, and I started to worry about her hand on my knee, which is to say now I felt superior and judgmental, even as I then pretended to relive the experience of Katie's death each time she flashed the light into my eyes.

Why was it so hard to submit to her method? Why did I adapt it into some inferior pantomime? It seemed a matter of accountability. I wanted feeling in a therapist, but also detachment. I wanted someone who did not seem to worry whether I got better, who facilitated my own self-cure rather than administered her own; a therapist who might abandon me at any moment because, really, I was doing this on my own, and I should be made to fail if I was not sincere in the effort. In this way I felt very Catholic and midwestern. Perhaps the goal of therapy was not to get better at all, but rather to sustain one part of the conversation, so that it continued through and after Katie's death. And yet, if that was the case, then Katie's death was the only occasion to continue the conversation.

Which was the real interruption I sought to clarify with a therapist: loving and knowing Katie or living after her death? In the beginning I could not distinguish between the two. Mine was only one side of a conversation about tics and habits, familial awkwardness, the shared generational tensions into which everyone escaped or submitted through marriage. Here I was now, after my marriage to Katie, and the story still had so many beginnings and no end.

Sometimes, in therapy, it seemed as though I was speaking only in abstractions. In my Marriage, Independence accommodated Need very well and was rewarded with Companionship and sometimes even Approval. I was once the Husband, and now I was the Widower. In fact I was the Young Widower.

Were these categories helpful? I made a claim to Katie based on memory. After her death, that claim seemed as hypothetical as anyone's. The high school boyfriend who checked himself into the hospital after they broke up. The girl who spread Vaseline across her windshield and bumpers, then kept the economy-sized jar out on her dresser until Katie came by a few days later to visit. The coworkers, friends, family members, and strangers who paid their respects at her wake and funeral and who continued to be in touch in the weeks and months that followed. They all loved Katie, I believed, even as she had chosen me. Nothing that followed could change the fact of our marriage; our marriage, now, that was ended.

Were these connections and associations real? Could I really follow one perspective so clearly that it might interconnect everything and everyone to Katie's death?

Katie's death is the Large Hadron Collider, I told the therapist. *It reveals in a fraction of a fraction of a second the nature of the universe, ourselves, the world around us. What happens in an instant to create or destroy everything else.*

The therapist said, *Let's talk about the pills. Do you need one every night? Could you try every other night for a week and see how you sleep?*

I thought, *What would be the point of lying to my therapist?*

What I meant to say was I had no intention of letting go either the ritual or its significance. If I took the pill, then I was sick. If I was sick, then I was still traumatized. If I was still traumatized, then I still missed Katie. If I still missed Katie, then I still grieved. If I was still grieving, then I needed therapy. If I needed therapy, then I should not yet leave Indiana, my nieces, my small room in the back of the house, next to the truck driven by the brother-in-law with whom I talked less and less.

Was I really still grieving? Did I want to leave Indiana?

I said, *I'll give it a shot.*

Many friendships complemented the steady slog of grief. Some did not. Those conversations with friends that began with consolation, privation, and the absence of sense sometimes found no transition to the stuff of regular living. They began instead to repeat themselves and gradually became silent. I missed some of those friendships very much. I told myself, *They are foul-weather friendships.* They are good only in bad times.

All lives existed now on some continuum of self-sympathetic comparison, beyond any coincidence of fact and imagination. Wasn't this the terrible secret of grief, the hedge against which so much talking, therapy, and time could find no certainty to obscure? I could survive anything. I could walk away from anything. There was no underlying structure, no interconnection, no resolution so permanent toward which we all had to work collectively. There was, in fact, no empathy for Katie's death, her absence in my life, or the tragedy of witnessing it. There was only sympathy and, after a short while, omission and silence. Our choosing or not choosing to be together.

My conversations with the therapist came to concern equally Katie's death, our marriage, my personal history, and my sense of a future. I could especially see the lens widening in how we talked about the present. It made a neat loop we overlaid onto the past until the connections became particular and vivid. We paused our sessions less frequently so that I might cry. We talked frankly about the rest of my life and how it continued, sometimes unremarkably, regardless of my sense of intention.

Grief was a perfect wheel. I turned it, again and again, with the hope of finding either its beginning or its end. I knew better. Therapy offered no permanent consolations after Katie's death. Together, the therapist and I could not animate or reclaim Katie, and if I only remembered her selfishly, bringing forward only our best selves, then I risked losing her entirely. And yet, I *felt* better to know that grief was itself both end and beginning. I observed it closely and learned to make testament to it. I tried to resist the perfection of Heracles, who sacrificed all he loved to become immortal. I tried to embrace, often with mixed success, but perhaps some sense of optimism, what the poet Yvor Winters made Heracles to say well after the fact: *This was my grief, that out of grief I grew.*

The advantage of therapy was that it was good for people who liked to talk about themselves. I excelled at therapy.

I found therapy useful for articulating ambiguities and narratives, for revisiting personal challenges. I had no idea whether I was a good person; if I was doing enough to honor Katie's memory; how to live with Katie's death; what it meant that the family I lived with was changing; whether that was somehow my fault; whether I had wronged my parents by not encouraging them more; if I was a lousy widower, son, brother-in-law, and friend. I thought we might sort some of it out. Which is to say, I worried about everything, as I had worried before Katie's death.

Ed came home from a consultation with my therapist and said, *Maybe I need to see a different therapist.*

More and more, we seemed settled into exclusive forms of grief. In therapy I felt ambitious. I wanted to understand more; to make better connections between my life before, during, and after Katie's death. There was a deep flaw in this ambition, and it took years to realize it, but the process kept me active and purposeful in the moment, and I appreciated, however willed, the sense of continuity.

I started a memorial foundation: paperwork, fees, applications, phone calls. Everyone in Katie's family and my family joined the board. We traveled together to Katie's graduate alma mater and awarded our first scholarship. I made a logo and a website, wrote by-laws and articles of incorporation. The government sent an official letter of designation. Then the foundation's promising start became something to argue over. Did Katie's father have more influence in the organization than Judy? Could we take construction crews to Mexico and build houses? Katie had once driven past a children's camp in central Illinois on whose board a cousin sat; couldn't we give them several thousand dollars to make renovations in her honor? A sense of hierarchy clouded our interactions. Who should be making these decisions, Katie's widower or Katie's family? We protected ourselves with distance, until what followed became a series of no-win scenarios. Was it really "Katie" to ask people for money, and should we risk going belly up? Could we hold the fun run in her hometown, and was it "Katie" to solicit local sponsorships? Wasn't it awkward to keep inviting family members to attend our events, when we knew they might not want to come? Was it "Katie" to take them off the list and so risk alienating them?

I thought, *In-laws are always outlaws.*

I thought, *A loving widower does not stop talking to the family of his dead wife.*

I ran across one strip mall, then the next, toward the regional branch of a national bank. I had no cash in my wallet to pay the cost of therapy, and my session would begin in minutes. I thought, *If I do not pay the therapist, then she will not see me; if I miss one session, then she might not schedule me for another one; if I miss therapy, I will regress; I will lose my progress; I will collapse.* This was my fear: disrupting the process. I had faith in it. I ran across the strip mall so that I might keep my part in it. Before most sessions I made a list of things to talk about it, but today, because I had no cash and I was running late, I would have to improvise the list. Would the therapist say I was not fully committed to the process? Would she say I seemed reluctant to get better? The ATM overhung the side of the bank building. I punched the numbers on the screen and waited. I made a fist with my hand so that it would not shake. I ran back across the parking lot, toward the office, and when I could not run, I walked. I stepped carefully between cars and tried to catch my breath. I ran again. We would start the session late, I thought, if I arrived there at all. Even that afternoon I would not describe the experience of Katie's death in terms of grief and witness. I would not think to say, until much later, that as I ran across the parking lots, I seemed to enact again the circumstances of Katie's death. Instead, I would wonder at my failure to generate a list and try to hide my shame. I would sweat and cough and try very hard to improvise a list of things we might talk about at the session.

After Katie's death, need did not always manifest itself in moments of desperate, semirehearsed spontaneity; in quiet accusations and a closing of the ranks; in incoherent, late-night phone messages that, the next day, no one seemed to remember leaving. The therapist said I should take my wedding ring off of my finger, put it on a chain, and wear the chain next to my skin, around my neck.

Did I want to hide these physical markers of widowhood? In the day-to-day, could I ignore Katie's death if it was not always in front of me?

I told Ed of my plan to stop wearing black every day, and he said, *You were still wearing black every day?*

I went with my niece to the chain store, and we bought the season's bold madras prints and bright ringer-tees. I took them home, cut the price tags, and folded them in neat piles on the bed. I took the black shirts—oxfords, polos—out of the drawer and stacked them on the closet shelf.

I tried to stop mentioning Katie in conversations about the past whenever I met and talked with new people. I made my references singular: my time in Bangladesh, my work in Romania, my graduate alma mater. Clean and simple, uncomplicated by clumsy elaborations—"my wife Katie who died seven months ago," "living with my in-laws from my first marriage, which ended after my first wife's death, which is why I'm in Indiana"—I made two versions of myself. Privately, one expressed grief. Publicly, the other elided it.

What could be expressed in moral terms—ambition, the pretense to tragedy—and what was circumstantial, incidental to our intentions?

In therapy aspects of Katie's life were made imperfect by its sudden end. A certain gravitas simplified our storyline. I could idealize Katie or be angry with her, but I less and less thought of her as a person, with a life separate from me. There was the death, our life together before the death, and my life after it. *The death*. Was this really how I was saying it now? As I pieced back through journals, letters, and emails, I wondered how much of what she had left behind would remain unsettled and how much had settled into fact and story.

I told myself I was investigating a life, but the inquiries seemed to have unclear methods and purposes. Wasn't another name for this scrutiny, the turning again and again, neurosis? I was trying to end Katie's life by asking questions. I was generating still more suffering, in order to put it on public display and then worry about it. Here was the benefit of therapy: everything was made to have two sides. The trauma of watching Katie die had a context. It became singular. Katie's death was neither expressly my fault nor anyone's fault. I was not exceptional. Everyone went to therapy all of the time, for all varieties of suffering, however real or imagined or trivial. Therapy said that a life would improve with witness and scrutiny, that meaningful change required a desire to change and the understanding of circumstance. Had desire always been so easily twinned with meaning? Witnessing Katie's death did not mean understanding the death, but rather its context; the terms of our life together, rather than its end. In therapy, living after Katie's death required arrangement, but not necessarily adjustment.

In the weeks after Katie's death, I learned to watch my life at the distance of a shared responsibility. I monitored it with the therapist and was relieved to defer, for her consideration, the worst judgments about myself. Days we did not meet, I walked out the front door of the house, plugged my headphones into an iPod, and turned in any direction. I sought out new streets and cul-de-sacs in doglegs from the main road but usually circled back. After a while, it seemed I knew every inch of the city limits, from the highway on one side to the park with the well on the other. If it occurred to me that I was penned in and mapping out the well-defined limits of a temporary place, I do not remember it.

At home I returned compulsively, hungrily, to the same few rituals. When there was no anniversary, birthday, holiday, death date, I borrowed the emotions from songs, television shows, novels, documentaries, photographs, movies. The gestures of grief seemed separate of the feeling, foreign and terrifying again, something I wanted to both guard against and not let go. I thought, *I would rather run back our life together to any moment we might not have stayed together and follow it instantly to here.* To make a different kind of gap, then close it.

If I had chosen one of the other two therapists in Indiana, would I seek now cure—lasers, prayer, medication—rather than accommodation? Would I understand as well, if differently, Katie's death and her absence in my life?

I lived for thirteen months in Indiana. After I left, my room next to the garage was converted into an office. Filing cabinets and a large desk were moved into the corner. The bed was moved into the basement. The carpet was torn up, and the exposed wood was finished. At first, when he lived in the house across town, Ed would sneak back into the house to reclaim power tools, amplifiers, albums, a weight bench. One weekend Beth hired an industrial dumpster and loaded all of the extraneous crap from the house into it. A truck came to take it away. Large spaces in the house were now exposed so they could contain other things and be arranged again.

Erasing the Room

1.

The hallway outside my room in Indiana was narrow, well lit, and tiled in every direction. Most nights, I was terrified to enter it. I knew where it would take me: into the kitchen, past my bathroom and the laundry nook. There were forty-one parallel tiles on the other side of the door, a cat, two dogs, and five family members coming and going. I stood on my side of the door, imagining it held back a world all day filling with halved distances, closing the gaps between places where I felt safe. How many steps would it take to summon our old apartments in Bucharest, Chicago, and Miami? The mountain where I had watched Katie die?

A lamp near my window reached a shadow most of the way to the closet. Someone had always just mowed their lawn, and in the darkness the scent filled my room. It smelled nothing like Romania. I could imagine, then, that Katie had died months, even years earlier, or that she had died someone else's wife, or that we were again visiting Indiana together, as we did most summers, and in a few days would leave together and resume our interrupted life. I would lie on the bed and wait for the room to fill with thick fog: quieter sounds, deeper breaths, a sense of fumbling toward familiar places.

Once, after I had taken a sleeping pill, I stumbled into the hallway and then the laundry room, locked the door, and caught my breath. I stood there awhile. It was hard to open this door, too. I imagined that I was playing a video game, stranded on a floating tile, waiting to time my jump back to safety. I understood that there was a finite period of time to get myself back into bed, before the pill erased the room entirely. So the room, too, was part of the game. Get inside before the clock runs down, and everything falls off the screen.

Summer mornings in Indiana were humid and sunny. Dampness took off the chill. I awoke under a sheet, earplugs in, my two cats nestled on either side. I felt relief to see light under the blinds and to hear the kids watching television in the kitchen. I had disappeared for the night and now I was back. I became adept at holding in my mind this first instinctive reaction to the world. Fractions of seconds, a few seconds. I awoke grateful and happy to be alive.

Sleep during the day was impossible. My mind was always snapping my body to attention just as it shut down. I would sit on the screened-in porch, under the ceiling fan, and try to read one of Katie's favorite books. There is a passage near the end of The Razor's Edge where the hero, Larry Durrell, cures his friend's crippling migraines through guided meditation. The friend holds a Tibetan coin until it drops from his fist; the pain subsides, and the friend is restored to health. A few times I held a Romanian coin in my fist and imagined a great ball of light opening out into the room and consuming, gradually, me, my grief, Indiana. Nothing.

I managed one side of consciousness vigilantly, meticulous about therapy and recovery; I tried to understand how trauma affected the body and brain. The other side of consciousness—sleep— remained vulnerable to unwanted memories and intrusions. I could not guard against or control them. Sleep was a transaction whose terms I negotiated daily. What did I need to sleep. What would make it less scary. Transitional spaces lost their boundaries. Often, I would dream in some symbolic interchange with the circumstances of Katie's death: trying to pull a friend out of a sinkhole, catching my nephew before he fell off the bed.

Sleeping medication altered the terms of my grief. It diminished my sense of need, absolved me of guilt and anxiety, and threw a broken switch, which stuck. It was comforting to take a pill, complete the routine of each day, and then transform the coming night. It was terrifying to think about the dreams I might have if I didn't take the pill. How would my mind accommodate its obligations to memory and imagination without the filter of chemistry? However hard I thought about it during the day, come bedtime, sleep was made to seem, again, inevitable.

That first year, I had two recurring dreams about Katie's death.

In the first a pack of wolves arrives slowly from a great distance to attack someone I don't know. I can hear them whimpering, they move quickly, their bodies are lean and mangy. They seem to come at once, full of implication, never ending, like ants toward a sugar dish. Sometimes, I wake before their arrival or just after the attack begins. Other nights, I try to make an emergency call on a cell phone that doesn't work, or I follow the wolves to reclaim the body. It is mangled and bloodless, smooth to touch. I carry it through a city.

In the second dream I am again a Peace Corps volunteer, back in South Asia after Christmas. The staff, teachers, and superintendent from the teacher's college greet me and take me to my old room. My bed, radio, ceiling fan, bamboo table, and bookshelf are exactly as I left them. There is a yellow quality to the light and dust everywhere. Or, it is evening, and there are only a few hours to arrange things and then get to the market to buy food and water. Katie is coming the next morning on the overnight bus. She is thin and young, tired but smiling. I can smell the baby powder deodorant that she used to wear, the sweat dried on her skin after a long bus ride. This part of the dream is brief but also the most fully present; the sense of time is uneven and particular, the feelings urgent but unfocused. I need to explain things, I think, and quickly.

We sit on the bed, or she sits on the bed and I sit at my desk, or we walk together across the lawns of the school, deserted now. No cows, mosquitoes, or students. We are alone on the small campus. The hostels are boarded over, and the grass is thick. We do not have to watch for sinkholes and snakes. We can walk a great distance in no particular direction. As we talk, there is never a moment of dramatic confrontation about my continuing life, and this almost always disappoints me: in the dream neither of us seems especially determined to fight for the life we had together. It does not occur to me to warn Katie about her death, its violence, the few simple things either of us might have done to prevent it.

As I wake, I lie in bed thinking how simple the story is, how easy it will be to retell. I believe that I am committed to a single fidelity, a sequence, and that a sense of continuity is preserved in the waking world. This is tidy and only partially true.

There is an act of withstanding that relocates violence entirely within the realm of imagination. There is a locus to violence that, like grief, makes a single point in time stretch in every direction.

It can be named, managed, and witnessed. In the first dream, restoration—claim the body, take it to the proper place—precedes my obligation to the dead. Katie is the occasion for a dream into which she never enters. In the second dream, Katie is recognized but not accommodated, welcomed but not invited. I am grateful to see her and even to seek her out, but only on another continent.

When I meet Katie in the dream, I explain myself without worrying about the consequence to either past or present. When I do not meet her, explanations are made to whoever is listening. In both versions of the dream, an account is rendered in the negotiated terms of a witness and a survivor who is married again. It is my mind and heart that resist complication. Whoever expresses them to me, they are my terms and my corrections.

2.

Leaving the therapist's office, need for sympathy induced a certain vertigo. Shame often accumulated in the silence after our shared witness. When I was critical of myself or our life together, I saw less of what Katie and I had loved and valued. There became no high ground on which to stand at a distance from the day's event, from Katie's death and our life, and say, *No, it did not happen that way at all. There is a part of this we cannot understand together.*

Wasn't shame the means for self-transformation? Shame required sacrifice and contrition. It was a grammar for failed self-regard that terminated, always, in affection and distance. I sought it beyond hunger and rational thought, beyond even feeling. Rather than high and open ground, shame was, finally, the closed room only I could enter. I groped at these walls, too. I held myself up in the darkness, knowing I could find my way again and again to it. Whoever I invited, however I explained it, the walls were near and would not press closer.

When I had called Judy from the mountaintop, she did not demand explanation or story from me as I feared she might, and she did not indict me for the fact of Katie's death. Instead, she offered to help me. I felt gratitude for her kindness in the days that followed. I tried to reciprocate it. The day before the funeral, Judy and I walked to a park near her house, where I again told her the story of Katie's death, this time more slowly and in great detail. I paused to make explanations, to clarify as best I could the parts she did not understand. There were not many. Above all, she loved her daughter and admired Katie's courageous life. That life made sense to Judy because no one else could do it as she had, or so well.

Mostly, Judy struggled to piece together the narrative of the afternoon. How we had stayed on the mountain so late. Where we meant to go that we could not wait until morning to hike there. Was my gratitude part of the story I told Judy about Katie's death? It seemed awkward to include it, as though I would only shift the tone back to me. This wasn't therapy. My purpose was not entirely my own. And yet, my understanding of the night was incomplete without my gratitude. My feeling for Judy, and my need for her understanding, was a fixed part of the story I now told. I wanted her to know everything. I knew Judy very well.

Wasn't my failure to save Katie's life the part of the story that neither of us was particularly eager to articulate? However I told the story, Katie had left *me* on the trail. *I* had hiked back to find *her*. *I* had gone for help when *she* asked me to do so. *I* had *returned* to her when no one else would: to wait with her, and then stay up all night with her body, certain to move it across a country and city, two continents, an ocean, glaciers and wheat, and her hometown, to bring her to Judy, as I knew Katie would have wanted.

I ran these emphases over in my mind. Each time I failed to find in their articulation the courage I hoped they might retrospectively express.

It was defensive to make such distinctions. No voice argued with me. Doctors, friends, and family members agreed the mind was a mechanism of self-preservation. The body submitted to the mind.

I did what *any rational thinker would do* and should want to do. *What I had done.* And yet, for all of my explanations, I understood clearly my failure. I hated to feel forgiven. I needed to feel ashamed—that I had moved through mud that night and felt nothing—if only so there might be *some* moral component to what had happened.

To a sympathetic stranger, I *did not understand how things really worked in nature.* To Judy, even, I was *too hard on myself.* Wasn't this what I could do best as witness and survivor: to make the fact of Katie's death undeniable, vivid and void of euphemism? In every telling of it, I might do something very generous to assuage the curiosity and terror about which any listener might otherwise feel some hesitation to inquire too closely. I did not want the story of Katie's death to be only the story of my having watched Katie die. And yet, weren't my emotions that night exceedingly relatable? Outside of anatomy and logic, how else might I make the imagined experience vivid and particular to someone who was not there?

Shame made me feel powerful. It allowed me to practice an exacting and particular neurosis. I played the role of constant failure. Shame permitted evaluation to fill in the gaps, arguing by proxy that, really, it didn't matter whether I had failed Katie, so much as to what extent and in which continuing ways. Shame made me both feckless and omnipotent, a coward with questionable motives, the rube who couldn't help not knowing better, the mastermind who willed from a chaotic mountaintop the narcissism of ardent regret.

3.

Katie had been a finalist for a different fellowship that spring, one she did not ultimately receive. With its support, rather than Romania, we would have spent parts of the year in four cities: Atlanta, Spokane, Cincinnati, and Washington DC. Katie would have interned at different departments in the Centers for Disease Control and Prevention. I remember thinking at the time it was good that she had not received the CDC fellowship. I had never especially liked Atlanta. I did not want to move every three months to a new city. I certainly did not want to visit her in these cities while living in a different one. If we were going to move, then I wanted to live abroad again. Unlike Romania, I could not locate Spokane on a map.

After Katie's death, I understood my reluctance meant I had wanted Katie's application to fail. I was ashamed to tell her so. The fact of wanting anything, I thought, rather than providing the unconditional support of a loving spouse, meant I had been controlling, manipulative, uncharitable, petty. When, instead of the CDC, Katie accepted the fellowship from the Coca-Cola Foundation that placed her in Bucharest. I was excited for our new adventure.

In fact, our departure had been anything short of dramatic or poorly considered. We talked, planned, hedged, hoped, and waited. We rented storage units and bought traveler's checks. Katie flew to Romania while I stayed behind in Miami a few weeks to pack our things. I loaded boxes into a U-Haul and drove them to our North Miami storage unit. I sold furniture on Craigslist. Katie had sealed the contents of her drawers and desk into boxes I stacked indiscriminately alongside the rest of our apartment: dishes, silverware, books, clothes, jewelry. When I unpacked those boxes, much later, I was surprised to see how hastily Katie had filled hers. She had not put much planning or forethought into the effort. The day before my flight, I crated the cats and dropped them at the international cargo terminal of the airport. Katie claimed them the next day, after they cleared customs and animal control, and a few days later met me at the airport.

In Indiana shame made no place for either this rather pedestrian sequence or our last life together in the United States, before we left for the Eastern European frontier. But I could shape it until it became, even as I knew better, a crude prediction of our last year. In my telling, all objects were artifacts of our recklessness. The rooms of our life were bright and various. Fate might interchange anecdote and confidence, so that both might seem still vital as the conversation continued.

Katie loved superhero stories. In the early summer heat of our cross-country drive from Chicago to Miami, we had stopped in Georgia to watch a matinee showing of the *Spider-Man 2* premiere. Through six hurricanes our two years in Florida, she read the first five *Harry Potter* books by emergency flashlight. Flipping through the DVD extras from a season of *The West Wing*, we marveled at how small the set was, how wide angles and high color made a distracting polish across each scene's thin wood and fake glass.

Really, Katie loved the superhero backstories. How any ordinary person would be revealed in the secretive reluctance of talents—Vincent D'Onofrio in *Happy Accidents* and Sawyer from *Lost* were particular favorites—well in excess of his ordinary, even hapless affect.

Here was what I knew about the heroes Katie loved: they were compelled by a persistence of failure. They did not quit until they were beaten. They gave all they could, beyond the perfection of their conflict, to willingly die. Most were trained to die and made to feel mortal for their exception, while the rest, in the moment, discovered an infinite capacity for the suspension of rational judgment. Whom they left behind, and how, and why, were beside the point. The best heroes were transformed by death. The rest became martyrs.

My desire to remember Katie was many things: devoted, empathic, needy, self-important, lonely, critical, nostalgic. It was not heroic. I was ordinary. Even this acknowledgment was an excuse for the fact of my helplessness. Time and again, I was asked to explain my witness of the events of Katie's death. Time and again, I offered also the explanation of my limited action, the occasion of my nonintervention, as though witness were a part of the sequence of facts. I was slippery. I dodged, in the everyday, the fact of my cowardice, but in my accounts to strangers, I bided my time. I did not change.

4.

A year after we moved to Miami, my first published poem appeared in a small literary journal. Before its publication Judy asked for a copy of the poem. I sent it to her in the mail: "Crepuscule." I had picked the title from a thesaurus. I was in the habit then of titling my poems with obscure words: "Zugzwang," "Lepidoptera," "Scumble." The poem was eight short lines, a plainspoken tribute to dusk.

Judy printed and framed the poem then placed it on her mantle. She asked me to sign it, and I did. We talked about the meaning of the title, "Crepuscule," then the meanings of some newer poems I had sent to her. I loved sharing my poems with Judy and the instant, kindhearted encouragement she offered me. *That*, she said, *anyone might sit down to write a poem, then share it with the world, is a pretty wonderful thing.* It was easy to talk about writing with Judy. She wanted only to know that I loved what I did. She loved that Katie and I seemed so happy.

After Katie's death, I wanted to find in my life in Indiana a sense of myself living still as her husband. I could not always do so. To understand the difficult oppositions between that first life and the life that continued in Indiana, between the obligations of marriage and degrees of individual freedom, meant acknowledging that on some level I had chosen to live in Indiana—I was not a victim there—just as my obligation to Katie was a choice, rather than a contract. It followed, like any obligation born of traditions, the clear limits of self-preservation. There were, in the end, exempt clauses—divorce, annulment, custody, common law—and ends to status—widower, divorcée—the distinctions of which, after a period of time, made the marriage an idea as fixed and uncertain as death itself.

In Indiana I saw no wedding ring, bedroom furniture, kitchen and chopping board, closet filled with work clothes. I lived in a borrowed room with simple things. What troubled me, increasingly, was not whether Katie had liked our marriage during her short life, whether she felt shame or relief at her place in it, but whether, when she left it, against her will, before her time, she might have wanted her absence to be sustained outside of it and then, for how long. I could not reclaim the lost present, any more than a blessing might reanimate Katie's dead body.

During a snowstorm that January, I taught my nieces and nephew how to play chess. My parents had sent them two hand-carved sets for Christmas. I lined the pieces in order on the table and showed how each one moved, running the axes across the board.

Katie and I played a lot of chess, I said, *especially when we first moved to Chicago.*

We played together almost every day, after school, for the next two weeks. My nephew, the youngest, played it like checkers until he got the hang of it. The older niece could see several moves in advance, while her sister played a more intuitive game.

I had teased her once about a boy in school she liked. I called the house phone and pretended to be him, throwing my voice. Even after she knew it was me, she played along. For a while she called my cell phone, throwing her voice, pretending to be Ben.

One afternoon we decided to watch television, rather than play chess. We made popcorn and flipped through the cartoons. We walked to the strip mall and picked out a couple of movies for the night. We never talked about Katie on these walks, not directly. But a kind of alliance was formed by my presence in the house, in exclusion of the rest of Katie's family. The first time I left the house, six weeks after Katie's death, to visit my brother in Chicago, I returned home to find a painting on my bed. My younger niece had painted eight black planets on a white canvas, extending out from a black sun. There were a few small black stars. In large black letters, along the bottom, she had painted KATIE.

5.

In Bangladesh we took mefloquine pills as a guard against malaria. The medicine was mildly psychotropic and had the effect of making our dreams incredibly vivid. I jerked the wheel of my car hard to the right and turned donuts in the parking lot of a grocery store near my high school. It was raining, and the tires had the effect of changing the color of the water. Or, I walked the near-north neighborhoods of Chicago, in winter, until I arrived at the Music Box Theater. I could never make out what was playing on the marquee, and I did not go inside. I would stand by the ticket window, waiting for a friend to arrive. I would wake feeling young, overwhelmed, homesick. I did not want to have these dreams, or I wanted to dream about Chicago and my hometown but feel ambivalence, not nostalgia.

During our Peace Corps training, I lived with a host family, near the train station. I would walk with a friend to the college where we took language and culture lessons. We followed a train track as we cut across the city. We shared a love of movies and passed the time by quoting or reenacting our favorite scenes. Once, passing through a sparse winter vegetable market, he looked at me, smiled, and said, "This might be the garden spot of the whole country! People may travel hundreds of miles just to get to this spot where we're standing now!" I knew the movie—Butch Cassidy and the Sundance Kid—but could not remember the end of the quote. I wanted to participate, so I thought of another line I knew, from earlier in the movie. "Can't swim? Hell, the fall will probably kill you!"

That spring—our fifth year together, the second of our marriage, our last in Miami—hurricane season arrived early. It brought six storms between April and November. After the first storm, I stood

on the screened-in lanai. The late-day heat had given way to mosquitoes and swamp bugs. We had spent all day and night in the
same small room. I didn't really know why I was angry with Katie.
It was evening in Miami, and it would rain again, all night, warm
still. I heard the whir of the air-conditioner drying out the room.
Outside, the bay receded for the night under docks and back into
the mangrove. Katie was tired and wanted to sleep, but I insisted
we stay awake. *We should end the fight,* I said, *and not go to bed angry.*
What more was there to say? We were resigned and wary. We could
no longer articulate simple points, the cause of our anger, and how
we might resolve it. We climbed into bed, finally, and Katie fell
asleep quickly, and while I insisted I was too angry to sleep, soon
I slept, too.

I woke in the middle of the night, and the anger was gone,
replaced with shame and guilt and the vague hope that it might all
have been a dream, that something spectacular and outside of
myself could magically fix things. *No,* I told myself, *I should be stub-
born.* We were making a precedent, and I needed to hold my ground
that next morning. It would matter who first apologized. Later, a
friend would say it very simply: either be happy or be right. *What's
the point of being happy,* I said, *if I'm not right?*

That night I rolled into Katie, and, half asleep, she pulled me
close. We slept like that a while. When we woke, the room, the city,
even our marriage were exactly as we had left them. Stone faced,
we stared across the bed a while at each other.

Now, Katie said, *here is the problem with being good at words.*

Cognitive Bandwidth

The occasion for my arrival in Indiana, Katie's death, yielded to the everyday affections of family life. However provisional, I felt I belonged there. I liked it.

We drove across town to picnics and amusement parks; walked to Friday-night dinners at neighbors' houses to watch movies and play board games; took our time at the franchise coffee shop, the Goodwill store, and the ice cream parlor, even the sporting goods outlet, where the kids bought me an olive zip-up sweater for Christmas. At home we made pizzas, pancakes, cookies, and tacos. We played guitars in the living room. We watched television in the family room. We put our feet on the sofa, our heads on the floor, and played a new game, Upside-Down Ball. We drove to the Broad

Ripple deli counter with the good fries, to the Indianapolis Museum of Art to see the original Hiroshige prints, to parking lots near the Riverfront walking paths or the orchestra hall across the street from the city's memorial fountain lit blue for football season and red for the basketball tournament.

I looked for my life with Katie in these new routines. In an alternate reality, dim with recognition, we still sat on that balcony overlooking Bucharest, talking about work and making plans for a future that would never bring us here. That year, even our life, seemed less and less certain. I sat in my room at night looking on Google Maps to remember the order of the city's monuments along my walk across the city to Katie's office: through the embassy district, past Revolution Square, then down along Unirii. I pointed the cursor at our apartment building and cropped the space around it until the screen would not magnify. The pixels went blank with warnings about restrictions.

All spring I biked the Monon Trail to the city limits. I stopped for coffee at the underpass by the public library. I sat on the lawn, in the midday sun, watching strangers and reading my book. After therapy sessions I biked a stretch through the wealthiest neighborhoods in Indianapolis, making a long and inevitable loop toward the state highway. It was an election year. Candidates conceded races and endorsed rivals. I followed the minutiae of each primary, cheering underdogs on both sides. I had no workweek, really, only an obligation to show up to teach business writing at the university twice a week. Those afternoons I did not teach, I sometimes met Ed for lunch. More often, I stayed home and made sandwiches with Beth, catching up on our days, books, music, neighbors, friends. When she returned to her home office, I disappeared into my room to write or to grab a jacket for another long walk.

I see myself there: resigned, confused, scared, and uncertain. And yet, in many ways, I am happy to feel so loved. A first glance shows my room, filled with the markers of grief and sorrow, narrow from window to door, austere, thinly walled. A room to which I retreat to grieve but also to prepare some public version of myself. More and more, I am anxious to engage the world. There are gadgets and trinkets on the shelves, workout clothes in the dresser, correspondence stacked and opened on the desk. Even in this temporary space, under exceptional circumstances, there is some uncertainty about the hermetic life. I have never lived in a house where I might linger in a separate room for hours without consequence or explanation. When the door is closed, I am uneasily alone.

More often, I leave the door open. I sit at my desk until one of my nieces comes down the hall to visit the cat, or to talk about her day, or to make fun of my facial hair. She sits a while in the plush chair by the window, waiting patiently for my attention. When I know I am being watched, I cannot take myself too seriously. I learn the names of friends and the limits of teasing. Not boys; teachers and neighbors are fair game. New music is downloaded and burned onto discs slipped under doors; movies are rented and watched and left by the television; board games and conversations continue on the dining room table for days. This familiarity, this winning closeness, cannot be a consolation for Katie's death, and yet, I cannot imagine how I might otherwise enjoy it so much. I am learning the rituals of a family that loves me. The place I hold in it for Katie becomes my own.

Sometimes I return to the house early from a neighborhood party, before dinner, out the side door from a backyard pool, where some half-finished movie is projected on the wall. Walking up the drive, I see the outline of my cats in the low windows off the garage, under dark trees. Maybe an airplane or two passes overhead, reflecting back the city's lights. And there I am: walking past the mailboxes, up the drive, and through the front door to make a sandwich in the kitchen, sitting down in the living room to watch television by myself on a Saturday evening. A straggling procession of eventual arrivers follows at a distance. I can hear them coming down the short cul-de-sac. I am not alone in the big house for too long.

Weddings and funerals, Beth says, *bring out the worst in families.*

We are sitting in the kitchen on a Thursday afternoon in September, talking about Katie's funeral and the year between her father Wylie's death and Katie's funeral. I had missed the memorial service for Wylie, and though Beth does not hold a grudge, I feel keenly in the months after Katie's death my tenuous absence. Yes, the timing was awful; money was tight; I was leaving to meet Katie in Romania for a few weeks with no sense of any job that might follow—all of this is true—but the real fault of my absence was a certain tone-deafness to the pain of a family member, my close friend, who lived far enough away I might reasonably comfort her in person, as I had when we visited that spring, at Beth's suggestion, to spend a few afternoons with her father after his move to hospice care.

I appreciated that you sent flowers, Beth says. *Some people didn't even do that.*

Katie and I had liked Wyle. He was a charismatic, generous man. He had a terrific skill for entertaining his grandchildren all day, then dropping them off at the house before dinner with sugar highs and full diapers. In his study he kept a display of American West tchotchkes that, after his death, sold at auction for a lot of money. Leather-bound encyclopedias with gold lettering and cream-stock paper lined the wall that faced the Sacajawea coins. Sacajawea, who guided the map makers west, then either died with her white husband of an unknown illness in St. Louis or disappeared across the Great Plains and lived alone for another sixty years.

Ed told his family that if they couldn't make it, it was okay.

Katie liked to say that Beth had married a hard man to love, and maybe I saw it more clearly that year, up close, living in his house. The terms of his affection were often singular, but winnowing. It was easy to follow Ed. It was hard sometimes to do much else. And this was the basis of Ed's growing frustration with his family: no one wanted to spend as much time outdoors on the weekend as he did; or exercise as frequently after work; or idealize the ascetic life, unplugged from the technology and waste of his long workday, in which he often found satisfaction by escaping to rural Kentucky, the rock-climbing gym, the church, or the guitar-filled basement, training one season for endurance sports and watching adventure television through the next. Ed needed exception from his life. He readied himself to prove on any mountain his fitness. Perhaps he believed, after Katie's death, that it could make his family safe. But his family wanted only to stay inside, watching screens, refusing nature, and practicing, from a great distance, his own vigilance.

But it wasn't okay! Isn't having a big group around you after a death what really helps?

One Christmas, visiting from Miami, while Katie was still asleep, Beth and I drove from Judy's house to the megamall with her daughters, to buy a coffee and a *New York Times*. It was 6:00, maybe 6:30 a.m. We had all slept on air mattresses in the living room, at least until the air mattresses had deflated; between trying to run the pump and settle ourselves onto sofa cushions, we had given up on sleep, finally, a little before dawn. We drove through town, out to the interstate. Really, we didn't expect any part of the mall to be open. The skeleton crew of baristas at the franchise coffee shop were blasting punk rock and dancing with each other. They had not expected us either. They comped our drinks. We wished each other a Merry Christmas. We left a big tip and then drove back to the house to open presents.

Planning Katie's services, talking to neighbors, visiting the church, cooking meals, watching all the kids. I like being helpful.

Hadn't I always loved escaping into the early-morning winter and driving in circles through the empty streets? Exurban Illinois was a bleak place, and being out alone made it feel like breaking some minor rule. It didn't matter I was out. It was only a matter of time before I returned.

It's nice not to only be the enemy who has stolen away the eldest son to my home in Indiana.

There was no sequence, no continuity around which Ed's affection might organize his family now. It was smaller after Katie's death. Its fragmented, vulnerable life might be the new norm, and I felt empathy for Ed's frustrations at having to acknowledge it. I listened, nodded, and hoped his contentions, however argued over, would eventually clear away. I watched them accumulate, until it seemed I could measure two broad, unequal portions: before Katie's death and after it.

How was that not my fault, too?

I'm pretty sure that, before too long, I'll be the enemy again.

Ed came to hear in the tone of his family's voices a talking back he did not like. He moped and stewed. The kids ignored it.

Fights became terrific and did not begin or end. They happened behind closed doors and out of earshot. The sudden absence of adult voices was striking, the eventual emergence from rooms and the continuation of routines uncomfortable. I felt guilty, by proxy. I hated conflict. I wanted everyone to stay fixed in some sense of themselves while I focused on grieving for Katie. Instead, I saw myself no fixed center for all of it. Ed believed there was plotting against him, a deep and persistent rejection of his values conditioned by a wife who brainwashed the children to enable the persistent agreeability of his ex-brother-in-law. Beth, on the other hand, hedged Ed's wildest ambitions of nature, deliberately perpetuating a routine—soccer practices, orchestra lessons, sleepovers, breakfast—that was all surfaces.

For a while, I smiled and tried to take everyone's side. I had no idea how much television Beth let the kids watch while Ed was at work. I agreed with Ed it would be fun to spend more time in nature as a family.

The night Ed made homemade organic cheese during an episode of *American Idol*, I went back and forth between the kitchen and the family room, cheering all sides. Then, I thought, *This is ridiculous*. What did I care who ignored whom and for what reasons? I watched *American Idol*. I hated cheese. The kids were so happy to see one singer go home from the competition, while the other moved forward to the next round. When Ed's back went out and he disappeared up the stairs, I did not get up from the sofa.

Everyone tried to take the self-cure. Ed went to Kentucky at a moment's notice or stayed late at night in the gym at the strip mall. Beth spent more time out of the house during the day and with the kids in the evening. She started working part-time in an office.

I was familiar now and less exotic. My routines in the house grated: coffee grounds down the disposal, parking my car at certain inconvenient angles to the garage, my cats, a space heater forgotten and left on in the room all afternoon.

I could say it another, less careful way. Perhaps I did not want to love everyone equally after Katie's death. Maybe I no longer saw an obligation to encompass the complicated fidelities of other lives. It seemed that, whenever I finally left, two realities would commence, both independent of me: the continuing life of Ed's family and the individual lives it contained. I understood I might become the scapegoat for certain alliances. I was implicated for both my arrival into a family and my departure from it. The fact of my leaving gave Ed an ample rehearsal for his own departures. A few months before the divorce, over tea, Katie's grandmother asked whether Beth was going to leave Indiana with me.

Let me revisit that failure again and hope to revive some connection between Ed and Katie, in order to better articulate my own complicated affection.

A blizzard shuts down the city. We are all home for days on end. Ed is eager to watch a video from college, in which he narrates a ski trip with a handheld camcorder. On a snowed-in road, in a used car, Ed points the camera at himself, then at four friends. Their faces are lean and dark with stubble, hidden behind sunglasses. Each time the camera turns back to Ed, it takes a moment to recognize him. His voice is higher pitched in his youth. His tone is lighter. His words run in phrases packed with a skier's jargon I cannot follow. At one point the driver pulls over to the side of the road, to wait out the worst of the storm. The video stops and starts. Ed checks in periodically over the course of an afternoon to update their waiting.

Snow cakes the windshield in the video. Snow is hedge deep outside the window in Indianapolis. We are housebound and watching television, and I am watching a video with Ed and laughing when he laughs, because I like to see him so happy. But I cannot make his enthusiasm my own. I don't ski. I don't know Ed's friends or their jokes. I don't like mountains or wilderness, and I resent the danger he survives. It reminds me of Katie, and I think it would break Ed's heart to point out something so obvious. And yet, to say any of that to Ed would only ruin his enjoyment and shift the focus back to me, would only shock him from his own nostalgic and safe reverie back into a world we inhabit together because of Katie's death.

Ed runs the video a second time, and this time through I remember which parts make him happiest. I preempt his own laughs, repeating some of his narration. There is the effect of banter. It takes a great effort not to commence my own darkly ironic commentary. I wait for Ed and his friends to survive and continue their adventure. I know they will survive because I am sitting with Ed in his living room, watching his video.

I think of another movie from my childhood, in which two men debate the color of the apple on the Tree of Knowledge. What does it matter whether Eve passes to Adam a red, green, or gold apple? The apple is a beginning, a hinge from which follows everything: the Fall of Man, first sin, Cain and Abel, the Eve of Resurrection. It is motionless, ripe, filled with potential. To linger too long on the apple is to invest it with the worst kind of melodrama, to make the inevitability a kind of climax at which no real conflict is resolved. Only failure and postscript can follow.

I laugh with Ed because he is happy, but I am not happy. I am furious, sad, and scared. I feel trapped in a joke I don't know how to continue. I do not understand it. I want the feeling of our close-ness, rather than the acknowledgment and honesty that should probably follow it. This is my shortcoming and nervousness: my eagerness to get along. To say I see Katie anywhere in the video is to ruin his nostalgia and to impose on his joy the awkward shapes of grief and caution. My shapes. Ed does not look for them in the video. He sees only his happy, former self in a world where both his brother and Katie are still alive and far away, where his wife still seems to want to spend time alone with him, where she is still the girl who once loved him so eagerly she followed him everywhere. Everything was changing now. In the video whoever left his moun-tain continued a life in Indiana that had not yet become a family closed into separate rooms of a house, safely watching a different storm on television, waiting out the worst of winter.

My therapist uses the phrase *cognitive bandwidth* to suggest how I might think about what I can and cannot offer to the people in my life. At any given moment, 30–40 percent of my bandwidth is devo-tional: grief or trauma, Katie and our life together, her mortality and my own. Another 30 percent is functional: it gets me through the day, across intersections, to the gas station, out on walks, plan-ning lessons and meeting with students. The last 30 percent is dis-cretionary: I might entertain myself with movies and music, sit in my room with the door closed, talk with Beth over lunch, or bake cookies with my nieces and nephew. The therapist's point is that I can't do too many things right now, and I certainly shouldn't expect to do more than one of them well.

How present do I seem in any of these circumstances? Aren't they all temporary, anyway? I suspect sometimes it is my obvious detachment, my disinclination toward the world, that makes me so welcome. I remember best and most fondly those throwaway moments with my nieces and nephew; my lunches with Beth, eating French fries and cold curried chicken salad, talking about Katie, then swim lessons, the neighbors, then *The Office*. Sitting on the back porch talking about class rankings and math tests. Declaring unpatriotic a niece's classmate named "Tory." I make a welcome space for the spontaneous connections but also the concessions that sustain independent feelings and relationships.

My time in Indiana evolves in stages: grieving widower, live-in uncle, surrogate. I am less often the interloper. Afterward, I miss that certainty of fragile feeling and waiting to understand my place. Vulnerable and partially present, I live in small incidents of grief that bring us together. I float through major incidents against which I make no real progress. I am shaky but resolute. I am kind to whoever will have me. I expect very little, and we get along very well because of it.

Tying the Knot

After a terrific storm, I decided I was in love with a friend. I drove from the house to the public library, where I wrote a long email confessing my true feelings, which she no doubt shared. Katie was dead, and I missed being in love. Five months later I thought my friend would save me.

For the first time since Katie's death, I was bored. Those minor rituals of daily life that had once sustained the practice of hard emotion seemed increasingly mannered, sometimes canned. In my room, at night, I played the same three or four songs that I knew might overwhelm me and again make the pain of grief fresh and urgent. But I also listened to them in the car and at the burrito shop, while walking around the shopping mall or mailing packages to the friends who had sent small gifts all summer. I tried to think about grief in the past tense. I wanted to see myself as someone who had once grieved without consolation and who now knew how to live with grief in a continuing life.

Daylight Savings Time ended. Halloween decorations poked out of trash bins or became backdrops for paper turkeys and husks of Indian corn. Long evenings of streetlights, ice, and rain became the pitched, gray season. Because heat from the house did not circulate well to my room just off the garage, I purchased an electric blanket and space heater. In the morning I ran the shower to fill the bathroom with steam. Evenings, I drove with Ed and Beth to indoor soccer games or sat in the next room during Boy Scout meetings, looking over math problems with a niece and then running spelling lists. Once everyone headed off to bed, I filled out request forms online from the circulating desk.

That I was declaring my love electronically, and that time seemed of the essence, might have warned me off my task. Also, that I did not mention the plan to my therapist, my family, Ed's family, or anyone else I knew in my daily life. I did confide my secret in two friends, both men, who lived in Miami. For a while they even resented my friend for not doing the right thing, by which I understood they meant she could at least have humored me a little. I had been through something tragic. She was having boyfriend problems. Surely, there was common ground.

In the library that evening, parents with small children passed my desk. Teenagers in big coats and backpacks hurried to the far cubicles. Along the perimeter of the parking lot, a snowplow made great hedges of ice. From my window I could see the blacktop shining up under the overhanging lights: yellow hashes and numbers marking off each space. There was great potential in urgency, I told myself, and good reason to be hopeful.

I got to work. I took six or seven anthologies down from the stacks and made neat piles to hide my progress. I opened my laptop, my internet browser, and finally the email program. I loved the sense of risk, yes, but I also felt due whatever might come after grief. I was certain there was something. I had made my position redemptive and sympathetic for long enough. Now the world should come to me.

From the moment of Katie's death, I was an exceptional case for sympathy and comfort. Everyone said it. *No one should have to witness and accept so close to the start of a marriage the life and death of his spouse. No one should die so young.* To want to help to heal me, to try to mend the enormous tear in the social fabric through which I had fallen, made everyone decent. It was safe, even noble to love me.

Accepting that sympathy was a tricky catch-22. In order to grieve, I needed to leave the world for a while. In order to heal, I needed to embrace some part of the lives around me. I fashioned a continuing life in the molds of those who took me in and loved me. I participated in their lives, and in my participation I grew less wary of the world that had, in an instant, trapped and killed Katie. A gap developed. I cried at night, alone and behind closed doors, but during the day, with family and friends, I smiled. I was insistent, optimistic, stubbornly willfully and firmly engaged. I thought of the quote by Basho. *What is the point of trying to say everything to anybody?* I grieved for Katie's death. In different ways, we mourned the loss of her life. Our senses of grief were already long divergent. Katie's family took time and space to close ranks and reform the structure of a family in her absence. In order to heal, I needed to believe my grief at losing my wife and partner, magnified by the trauma of witnessing her violent death, was unquestionably the greater loss.

A few weeks after the funeral, I stood in the kitchen assigning tasks. Katie's nephew melted and whipped the butter. His sister packed brown sugar and sifted flour. Her older sister measured the baking soda and salt, cracked the egg. Their cousins chopped the chocolate bars into chunks, crushed the walnuts, tasted the batter. We all took turns measuring teaspoons of batter, and then we waited for the first batch to finish baking. Or, I waited and did dishes, while they watched television.

Judy and Katie's sister sat on the back porch, talking about divorce. I could hear their voices in the gaps between John Prine songs. Katie had loved John Prine. When we first met as Peace Corps volunteers in Bangladesh, she lent me her John Prine mix tape, which I only grudgingly returned, months later, after we had started dating. In the kitchen I kept restarting "Lake Marie," self-consciously playing it over and over, eager to telegraph the similarities between the girlfriend's murder in the song and Katie's death. I can't imagine what effect this had on Katie's mother and sister. I didn't ask, and I'm not sure they noticed. Ed might understand, I thought, but he was upstairs, putting his boy down for the night.

There was a terrific pile of dishes from dinner. We had made spaghetti together, following a recipe that Katie liked. I loaded soap into the dishwasher and ran it. I washed each of the pans by hand and laid them out on a checkered towel. It was warm out, but not so warm that we had to run the air-conditioning. I propped the front door to get a breeze going through the kitchen. I started "Lake Marie" again and took each of the coils off the burner. I scrubbed down the stove with big piles of Comet until it shined and smelled of bleach. I slid the coils back into place. The cookies were done. The kids came back to scoop them, still warm, and pour glasses of milk. They took a plate out to Katie's mother and sister. I made two more sheets of batter, ran the disposal, washed the bowl and spoon, dried the pots and pans, stacked everything into the cupboards, checked the cookies, waited.

I needed to keep moving forward. I wanted to slow down. I drank a big glass of whiskey. I went to the bathroom and dug out the anxiety pills a doctor at the embassy had prescribed. I had taken Katie to see John Prine and Iris Dement in concert at the Chicago Symphony Orchestra Hall for her twenty-seventh birthday. They had closed the show with a sing-along of "Lake Marie." The chorus is simple, Prine explained; you just sing "Standing by peaceful waters" over and over. At the concert only one person, sitting just up behind the stage, knew to yell out *Shadows!* during the last verse. *You know what blood looks like in a black-and-white video?* John Prine asked again, laughing, and we all yelled back, *Shadows!*

What was I doing in Indiana? These people couldn't heal me. John Prine couldn't heal me. Cookies and pasta were making me fat and keeping me awake at night. The pills and liquor felt good, like a heating blanket under the skin. I had a secret now; I was high, and no one else knew it. I would have to explain this to my therapist. I walked back into the kitchen. The kids had disappeared into the neighborhood, so I scooped the last batch of cookies onto a cooling rack, scrubbed the baking tray and poured myself another drink. The stereo sounded tinny now and too loud. I took out the John Prine, put in Lucinda Williams. I walked out onto the back porch and spent the rest of the night talking about the Fourth of July when Katie had beat me in her hometown's 5K Race for Freedom.

We did not always find the rhythm to share certain stories. Sometimes they became performances or claims to possession. It was possible that things had happened to Katie she never told me, that they knew and I didn't, but I didn't believe it. I couldn't. I had the full picture; I knew secrets, too.

The secrecy was corrosive. It was all we had to impose order. Together, we drank, told stories, and confided in each other. Individually, we named our grief and its cause in the most intimate terms. What we had lost. What we missed. Almost immediately, I hewed to a careful regimen of medications, therapy, and work. I sought, always, progress and action, accountability and disclosure. In an email to a friend I said that what mattered now, more than grief or teaching or even therapy, was that I knew *how to be a good uncle.* I started to want something that Katie and I had never planned for ourselves: a family. The idea that grief was singular, and that everyone mourned Katie's death in our own ways, on our own timelines, seemed too easy. Or, I saw it in much harsher terms. I was the widower, and I was taking care of my shit. Everyone else should, too.

I liked being married to Katie. In Indiana I realized I had also liked being married, period. I was, for the most part, pretty good at it.

I knew men who did not like marriage. They had not been eager to marry and felt saddled, even trapped, by its obligations. These were men who needed prompting to make the commitment, who resented social and family pressures and so made sure always to keep the door open just a crack. Intensive extracurricular hobbies abounded. Rock climbing. Ultra-marathoning. Amateur journalism. When they spoke casually about their marriages, they were seen as confident, even practical. When they forgot anniversaries and birthdays, the women who married and loved them declared that they were works in progress, models of a kind of manly independence, aloof in the most attractive ways. Perhaps these women sought also to crack the door a bit.

Did such men, widowed, feel liberated from marriage altogether? Did they miss it as much as I did? Was the prospect of remarrying as fixed in its hypothetical aspect? I wondered how they might make sense of the end of a marriage. Did everyone imagine doing it differently a second time, possibly better, seeking out a partner whose complement improved the marriage and both people as spouses? Could we idealize together marriage through the approximations and distances of grief? There were gaps now, intercut broadly with memories. If we tied the knot again, would we tie it about the same, or would we try to tie it tighter, faster, flatter, and more elegantly?

I say "tie the knot" to mean, of course, "get married": binding two lives together to make each life stronger, to distribute the stress and weight more evenly, to join (at least) two families.

The etymology of "tie the knot" is uncertain. Like any colloquialism its origin has grown less stable as its usage has become widespread. "Tie the knot" might mean to tie the first knots under a mattress, in the time before bed frames. To make a pledge together and so bind the words. To stitch ribbons into hair and mark oneself as a bride. To call forth a patriarch to stand in witness or perform a sacramental tying of cords. To bind the marrying couple's hands together, with a promise to break the knot only after the marriage has been consummated. To make sacraments in preliterate cultures. To weave a necklace of flowers and place them around a spouse's neck.

In Indiana I adapted my own meaning. I would tie a knot at the end of my life to whatever might hold it. I wanted to survive. I wanted to carry forward the best part of Katie's and my life and to begin to make an entirely new one, too. That these intentions might be contradictory was only later obvious; I sincerely believed that I could carry everything and everyone forward. As a young widower, I was indulged this fantasy because it made my survival seem more certain; healing was the important thing, and desire was a fine reason to heal. If I was still a man living in his brother-in-law's garage apartment, wondering what might happen next, then I also could not deny that I had survived Katie's death, able-bodied and young, the walking embodiment of an inevitable potential beyond grief. One day I would either leave the apartment or became *that guy* in the neighborhood, the cautionary tale, the one who moved in a while ago when things were really bad, then sort of hung around too long, never quite put the pieces back together, who belonged to that family for a while and now belonged to no one.

Katie and I met Ed and his family together a final time, in Germany, for a long holiday weekend in October 2006. We ate chocolates, drank wine, toured orchards and vineyards. We turned handstands in a field surrounded by sunflowers and mountains. We ate elaborate meals at the expense and generosity of a colleague to whom Ed had shown a kindness many years earlier. It was, in many ways, an idyllic trip. We flew back to Bucharest nostalgic already for the visit.

In the Carmel library I wrote plainly and with great affection. I had not practiced the tone in some time, but it was familiar enough. I meant to overlay onto the next relationship the carbon from the last. My hands shook as I wrote. I was excited. I thought of the scene in *Crimes and Misdemeanors*, where Woody Allen confides to Mia Farrow that he stole most of the material for his one love letter to her from Joyce. In college I had read Joyce's love letters to his wife. They were illicit, aggressive, shockingly erotic, and full of a vulnerability that made me uncomfortable. My purpose was noble, I kept telling myself. My project was restorative but also sequential. My friend was a cipher or maybe just the means to the end of knowing I was loved by one person more than anyone else.

Do I have that wrong now? Were my feelings real, honest, and uncomplicated by grief, separate of it entirely, and only now diminished, in the anecdote, because I know the effort failed?

Here is yet another advantage of widowhood. There is a tremendous restart button for widowers just below reality that few can deny each time it is pressed. Circumstance and time are finite measurements against the unrelenting situation of our grief. A spouse has died, and a joint life has ended, against our will. We did not choose either the death or the end of the marriage. We should not be here, and whatever we do next, we will not be held completely accountable. We are, after all, victims. We are responding to everything as best as we can. Please help us.

My life grew certain in Indiana.

No, that is not quite right. I *was* wanted in Indiana. I *did* belong.

In the most extreme moments of grief and boredom, our situation was not unlike playing very well on a basketball team. Within the space of five people, I was a surrogate, a trusted sixth man who could come off the bench and play quality minutes, spell the stars, and then sit back down and wait my next turn. I sustained meaningful friendships with people I loved dearly. I learned firsthand how families work, what good parenting is and can be. I sacrificed, contributed, and tried to play my role.

I was not a parent. I was hardly an authority figure. Usually I needed Ed or Beth to intervene and lay down the law when a niece or nephew was really out of line. I would make a joke of it, declaring with feigned exasperation that I was an adult and the kids had to do what I said. We all laughed. But teasing only covered the gap. I could do part of the job very well: games, homework, shopping, movies, trips to the park and mall. I had no idea, in the beginning, how to do the harder parts.

After Katie's death, our marriage became a fixed thing in the minds of everyone who knew us. We had been married until Katie died, which meant now that we had been married until the end of her life. The corollary was that if Katie had lived a long life, then we would have been married for a very long time. Of course, there was no real way to prove this logic, but there was also no way to deny it and certainly, in the beginning, few occasions to do so. I was the widower of a successful and loving marriage that had ended too soon. That it had ended with a bear attack in a foreign country, and that I had witnessed and survived the attack, only magnified the exception. Alongside the grief, depression, and daily maintenance that consumed my life and made its routines and obligations so challenging, I began to feel something very different. I was relieved of the burden of living a full life with Katie.

> Hi John,
> I'm glad you feel comfortable enough to tell me this. I would like to be equally honest with you, because that honesty has always been one of the hallmarks of our friendship, which I treasure so dearly. So I have to say that, no, I don't reciprocate your romantic feelings. I feel like I'm in love with my boyfriend. I do reciprocate the happiness of having such a close friendship, and I consider you one of my two best friends (and have since we met).
>
> I know "treasure" is a lame word, but that's how I feel about our relationship, our talks, our writing exchanges, all of it. If it was in me to reciprocate your feelings, I'd be a fabulously lucky girl, but for whatever reason, it just isn't.
>
> It's good to hear you say that you feel good telling me about this. And I feel good too. If you want to talk on the phone, please give me a call today, tomorrow or whenever.

It is redemptive to witness suffering that will not last. It confirms our hope for the worst part of morality, that something outside of ourselves might limit our intentions in and for the world. The individual life must continue, we hope, with its satisfactions and frustrations, understandings and appetites.

I had no idea how to continue the argument I had started with my friend—*Love me! No, really, love me!*—so instead I tried to win it. I pretended my friend didn't exist, and when that didn't work, I got angry at her. I started and ended phone calls abruptly, made thinly veiled jabs, edited the writing we shared with unfair criticisms. I returned en masse a series of books I had borrowed over the years. I was petty, and whenever I felt called to account, having overstepped the furthest line of decency and fairness, I had to only say "Katie," and everyone understood instantly that I was not well. These blunt frustrations of widowhood found sharp relief in the living world. It was intoxicating to feel anything.

The sympathies of grief did not extend beyond witness and consolation. I formulated elaborate arguments and justifications, explanations, and they all meant nothing. However eloquent, I would not win this argument. It was not an argument. We had no common terms. I had a tremendous sense of entitlement, but no purpose. The emphases of grief and widowhood up close were not persuasive to everyone or to every situation in which I sought an advantage. My marriage to Katie, her death and our life together, had little, if anything, to do with the trivialities of daily life.

When I was a kid, I often came home from middle school in a full panic, eager to confess to my older sister how certain I was that everyone hated me. Usually, she would gently correct me, maybe even patronize me, but she always found a way to tamp down the anxiety, at least a little. One time she looked at me a little while, sighed, then said, *John, they don't hate you. They probably don't even think about you. You really have to give a damn about someone to hate them.*

Most of Katie's friends stopped checking in. They could only manage so many conversations about the same thing. They had performed their duties as worthwhile and caring witnesses, but their emotional investment was not in me. They knew me in the abstract, as Katie's widowed husband, from a few visits over the years. After a while, I think, they simply missed and remembered Katie without me.

The healthy body does not grieve forever. It will not stay in bed all day, or refuse to work, or drink too much alcohol, or take too many pills. It is a highly adaptable organism. It lives in ice and grasslands, near oceans and rivers, on the sides of mountains and across long, dry plains full of wheat or sand. Like every appetite, grief gradually reveals its strengths and weaknesses, is reckoned with, evaluated, made even to yield to progress. If *healthy* is the subjective term, loaded with straw-man arguments and corrupted by the power of the expert, it is nonetheless akin to Potter Stewart's famous pronouncement about pornography. *You know it when you see it.*

I spent New Year's in Chicago, watching professional wrestling in my brother's townhouse while he and his wife went to a neighborhood party. Ben stopped by that evening to check in before going out with his ex-girlfriend. It was a thoughtful gesture, but I did not need to be saved. There was not much to check in on. I watched wrestling, then music videos and then the news, and finally the first fifteen minutes of a John Cusack movie. Around 10:00 p.m., I walked over to the party and talked with my brother's friends. The ball dropped. We sang. Somebody suggested we all meet the next morning at 6:00 a.m. in the courtyard, to make the Polar Bear plunge into Lake Michigan. I said I'd be there and set the alarm on my phone.

As I walked back to my brother's place, I wondered how cold the water would have to be to stop our hearts. Wouldn't it be ironic, and unfortunate, to have survived the place where Katie was killed, and to have lived the rest of the year in Indiana, only to die on New Year's Day, jumping through the broken ice? I looked online for answers, but the opinions were uncertain. I woke up late the next morning. I checked my phone. It was muted, and the alarm was flashing next to the message indicator. The neighbor was bailing on the lake jump but wished me luck.

In Indiana I looked for Katie at baseball games, saw her face or the shape of her body and the back of her head in shopping malls and foreign cities. But she was only there in passing, that damp and sweet smell of her sweat, her powder-scented deodorant and plain laugh. I woke from dreams that terrified me, in which she never appeared, and I was grateful for her absence.

When Katie was alive, the rope would slip through my hands, by the yard. I would think, we have all summer to fix this. It will get better. I meant well, and I would change nothing. Or, I would make sincere and complicated plans to change my lifestyle, to exercise more and not expect so much, to listen and communicate better. Always, we fell back into our old patterns. I was scared. I was well intentioned. I didn't know better. Or, I knew better and I failed. And then Katie died, and it didn't matter.

Rehearsals for Departure

1.

We take a cab to the outskirts of Bucharest to rent a car for the day. It is early spring, and Katie will die in a few months, but this morning I wonder how we might beat the weekend traffic. The plan is to claim the car, pick up Sara, and then drive two hours to Busteni. The rental office is seven stories up a Communist-bloc apartment complex. It retains a certain aura of unquestioning silence: marble pillars, travertine facades. We stand in the hallway, ringing buzzers and looking through the dark glass. Katie calls the company on her cell phone, but there is only a recorded message that we cannot translate. We retreat to the café across the street, lean our packs against the wall, and order eggs and coffee.

The office manager arrives a little before noon, hung over, eager to pick a fight. We need a car that morning. He will not have a car until late in the afternoon. We have no need for a car if it means we cannot leave town that day. He will charge the credit card either way. We will not pay him. Either take the car, or forfeit the deposit and fee. We sign the papers, load our things into the trunk, and head back to Sara's place.

At a supermarket we buy beef ribs, spices, potatoes, imported chocolate bars with chilies and candied fruit, bottles of wine. We dig a barbecue pit in the yard, then decide it will be better to slow down a bit and enjoy the afternoon. We are in no hurry. We have all day now to do nothing together. Sara finds some painkillers left over from her back surgery. She says they might take the edge off. We open the wine and watch three or four DVDs of a television show we like. We cook our dinner and eat it on her back porch, then walk to a nearby park to watch the sunset. We are tired again and a little cold, ashamed for having wasted the day like this. Sara asks to keep the car to run errands.

Calle Victoria is a straight shot between the two plazas nearest our apartments. We walk against traffic where it narrows into a single lane, past the park and art museum. We meander the neighborhoods. The streets and sidewalks are empty. We are still a little high. Katie holds my hand and swings her arms. We push the pace. We want to get home, to finish the day. A few minutes from the apartment, Katie suggests we stock up on milk and eggs for the morning. Sundays, nothing will open until late afternoon. At a fruit stand we buy fresh green apples, tart and a little underripe for the season.

Say, for argument's sake, we hire the car that morning and drive to Busteni or take the train instead. Say the rental agent is not sick. We are his only business, valued customers, in fact, for whom he has a late '90s Peugeot gassed up and ready to go. We make good time out of Bucharest, past the abandoned industrial parks and new farms, and arrive quickly in Busteni. We ride the cable car up the mountain, take photographs under the white cross at the top, poke around a bit. We find an easy day hike across the ridge and back, eat lunch, drink our celebratory beers on the porch outside the basement of the hostel.

We say that it was good to get out of the city and away from our routines. We should do this more often. On the ride down the mountain, we tell Sara about our weekend in Cali Manesti, for Katie's birthday, how we hiked near the sulfur springs and got lost on the farm, where I surrendered my shoe to a manure pile. Coming down the mountain, the cable car clicks and swings and stops for a while over the deep valley to wait out the high wind, but it starts again. We do not travel to Busteni three months later. Katie does not die on the ridge of that mountain on a Saturday in late June. The ridge is not made sacred by her violent death. A bear crosses the ridge that day and attacks no one. Instead, that afternoon in March, we cross Busteni off of our list. There are other parts of Romania to visit that summer, for my birthday, before we leave the country for good.

2.

I leave Indiana on a Monday in August. I have lived there, with Ed and his family, for a little more than a year. I pack my car the night before with everything I own, mostly books and a few pieces of small furniture I fit crossways in the backseat. I drive the kids to their bus stop and wait with Beth to give everyone hugs. The kids step up and head off to their new school year. Everyone is a year older. I haven't planned how to say goodbye to Beth or what it means to leave, except in the broadest terms. I am excited to be on my way. I have known for months that I will be leaving. We smile, say goodbye, and say goodbye again. I drive slowly down the block until, through the rearview mirror, my sister-in-law turns around to walk back into the neighborhood. I find the highway and play the mix of valedictory songs I have mapped out in advance for this moment. But the music feels too self-congratulatory. I start to feel guilty. I turn on the news until the signal fades past Lafayette, and when I am south of Merrillville, I call my sister-in-law and tell her I will be in Chicago in a few hours.

Earlier that week I drive to the storage locker and open the last boxes from Romania. I have promised Katie's family they can look through the boxes and take what they like, but before they do, I want to make sure I know what I am offering and that I will not miss the things they take. I separate out some of her clothes into one box, papers from her work into another. I find a Sudoku book where Katie has solved most of the puzzles. She has the habit of finishing one, then dating it, writing all over the page in an exuberant, loping script, "YES! TWO DAYS!" or "FINISHED!!!" Taken together, they make an informal calendar of our last year together, a record of one part of her happiness. I like seeing her handwriting again. I remember how she would write messages in the margins of the puzzles, passing them over my way as she was off to run errands or if one of us was talking to our family on Skype. I would find annotated Sudoku pages torn out of the book, all over the apartment. We even used them for scrap paper.

I drive north past Chicago. I stop at the grocery store a mile from the nature preserve and buy flowers. I park in the lot and make my way toward the place where we spread Katie's ashes. It is warm, even for the season, and there is not much shade. The flowers are coming out. All of the grass cut back from the path in winter has grown in thick, a little weedy. I can just make out the place where the ashes fell in a great clump, before we spread them by hand. I stand there a while, feeling good. We were right not to bury Katie in a cemetery. *She can go wherever she wants to,* I think, but that is too corny. *Let the wind take your troubles away,* from a song we both liked, is better.

A police officer stops Judy, Ed, and me in the parking lot of the subdivision across the street, the night after her funeral. *You should not be doing this.* It is late, the preserve is technically closed. The officer writes down our names, addresses, driver's license numbers. He gives us a warning about trespassing so close to a construction site. After he leaves, we sneak around to the back entrance. Fireflies are out, and crickets. After the summer rain, everything glows. The memorial site is a little more than a mile from that entrance, just past the clearing. We find it coming both ways on the path. We stand together and then spread out a little. We hug and put our arms across each other's shoulders, waiting to be done with our individual silences. The pile of ashes is hard, like wet cement beginning to set. All summer and fall I keep waiting for nature to get to work and dissolve it into the soil. In wintertime it disappears under the snow and ice, but come spring, I reach in and break it into smaller crumbles and throw handfuls of hard clay deep into the field.

3.

Ed takes me to the mountain bike trails just west of the city, a series of ramps and narrow, rocky paths with dusty turnouts and gravel pits. In his enormous red pick-up, we talk about the mountain biking trails in North Miami, where Katie and I went to graduate school: stretches of mangrove next to Biscayne Bay, steep hills and fences, the long slopes down to where the "diamond" trails began. We make our own loops across and back to the parking lot. I plug in my headphones and play Yo La Tengo's "Did I Tell You?" ("My brain's impatient, my heart's still willing to wait") over and over on my headphones.

I meet Ben in Chicago for the first anniversary of Katie's death. We have plans to fly to Bucharest, take the train to Busteni, and climb the mountain where she died, but I panic, and at the last minute I cancel our tickets. Instead, we walk the lakefront to Andersonville, past Katie's and my old apartment, and make our way to Moody's, where we play all of the Cat Stevens we can buy on the jukebox. Katie loved Cat Stevens, the *Harold and Maude* soundtrack especially. Leaving the bar, we try to take a shortcut east from Clark Street, back toward the lake, but we end up wandering into one alley, then into another, until we get turned around. Coming back out to Clark Street, we pass a party on one of the balconies, four or so stories up. A rock anthem ends, then the low hum of party chatter. As we pass under the side stairwell, clear as can be, the opening chords of "Moonshadow."

That first summer in Indiana, I lose Katie's wedding band. I wear it on the band of my watch until one day it falls off in the gymnasium where I play basketball with her brother, or disappears under the seat of his truck, or perhaps is lost in the burrito shop, after basketball, where I am sweating so much I take the watch off to protect the leather band. The watch is crystal action, wind-up, Russian made with Cyrillic letters across the dial. Katie bought it in Romania for me and gave it to me for Christmas. There is a small indentation where the ring leaves an impression on the finish, a crack in the leather. That night I stumble between rooms in the house, searching everywhere for it. I have taken a sleeping pill, and now I struggle to stay awake long enough to complete my search. I know I will not find it, that I am even probably looking in the wrong place, but I have to make a full effort. I need to believe that I have done everything I can to save the ring before I quit looking for it.

The ring that I lose is not Katie's engagement ring; I keep that one in a box on a shelf. It is not even the ring Katie wore on our wedding day. The ring I never find is white gold, slender as a ring tab. She purchased it in a Miami jewelry store to replace the original bands of thick titanium we had found online, whose weight she hated on her finger, how it clinked against everything she touched.

I tie the titanium ring to a rope twisted with a metal chain and wear it around my neck for the next year.

4.

Ion kills the engine and runs his headlights long enough for us to find the trailhead. The trees spread out down the hill in both directions. We walk shoulder to shoulder until there is no space between them, and when we stagger out seven or eight feet, Katie takes the lead and Sara walks behind me. I can hear the crunch of snow underfoot as I shine my flashlight on the back of Katie's head, then down at the path in front of me, then back behind me for Sara to see the way. I follow Katie. She keeps walking.

It is April 2007. Two months before Katie's death, six weeks after we do not drive to Busteni. Ion's bed-and-breakfast offers valet service from the train station, whatever the hour. His blue diesel pickup sits four across, with our bags in the back next to an enormous dog. The dog doesn't move, not even when the road narrows to a single lane between buildings and we stop to wait for oncoming traffic. The ride that night is uneventful. It takes less than an hour. We park near a turnout from the highway one, maybe two kilometers' hike from the cabin. Just follow the trail, Ion says. He will bring around the bags.

The next day, from his porch, we see houses up and down the ridge, but that night we seem only to walk deeper into a forest. Shouldn't we be there by now? I think. Isn't that a fork in the path ahead and, beyond that, another fork? I can smell wood smoke and charcoal, and periodically the snow seems to get deeper or shallower. We make as little noise as possible. Much later, when it is neither dark nor late, we agree a second possibility crossed each of our minds that we were terrified to acknowledge. We might never arrive at the cabin. There might be no cabin, no Transylvania, no Ion; only some elaborate Romanian hustle to fleece tourists and ex-pats, then abandon them in the winter mud and ice.

What curiosity plunges us so headlong toward adventure that we trust Ion's unmarked trail?

And then we are there, standing before a magnificent wooden palace filled with light, against which our flashlights make no shadow or intrusion. Ion and his dog stand on the porch, waiting for us. If Ion has passed us in the forest, he makes no mention of it. He invites us inside to shake out our shoes and hang our jackets, hats, and gloves near the fire.

Ion's wife has set out plates of cheese and cubed lard, which he now pares with his pocketknife and spreads on crackers. He ticks through a list of hospitality-laden questions, one after the next, practicing his English.

How did we like working in Romania?

Did we want to walk the next morning to the frozen pond at the edge of his property?

Who would like a nightcap of homemade brandy before he showed us to our rooms?

Ion explains that he owns all of the land from the road, past the cabin, to the mountain. He purchased it from the government after the fall of Communism, and now no one patrols the area. He has made a number of renovations. He is building new lots. He will make an enormous profit, and after the sale he will move back to his village and never work again. His daughter will study medicine or law in the United States. His neighbor's daughter is a junior at the Bowling Green State University in Ohio.

The brandy is bitter and burns in our stomachs. After a few more we are all pretty drunk. There is a back staircase to a room under the cabin where Ion keeps his dogs, and do we want to see them? We might hear whining in the night, and he doesn't want us to worry. He is conditioning the new litter for the following winter. If their coats grow thick now, more fur will grow back with the first freeze.

The door rattles on its hinges, even before he turns the deadbolt. He tells us to stand back. Then it starts: the low baying, or maybe it is howling, then the staccato yips of puppies intermixed with irregular barks. Some of the dogs are growing faster than the others, Ion explains, now that they are weaned. He keeps the mother inside the house, because otherwise she might feed only her favorites.

We wouldn't think to look at them now, Ion says, but these dogs will triple in size before spring. Every day they will eat their weight in raw meat. Then he will really begin to train them. He will isolate them from human contact to teach loyalty. Fully grown, this will be the only species of dog in Europe that can kill a bear: snap its neck and bring it right down to the ground.

He will sell the dogs to hunters and neighbors and make still another fortune. Tonight, though, we should stroke their soft bellies. We should reach between the slats and feel the heavy fur. They will not imprint on us; they will grow docile only if they learn to expect us every night. If this happens, Ion explains, then they will be useless. He might as well shoot them. These could be vicious dogs, Ion reminds us, but they make lousy pets. Tonight, though, their howling makes the cabin safe. Whatever walks toward the cabin that night, coming or going to the mountain, will let us be because of it.

5.

My last night in Indiana, after everyone has gone to sleep, I roll a notebook, a blanket, and some beers into a backpack. I drive to the storage locker, enter the code, turn the deadbolt, and open the box that contains Katie's journal. The cover is soft, black faux-leather. The pages are crisp but have a give toward the middle. They will soon crease. I have a little more than an hour before the gate will lock for the night. I sit in the hallway, under a row of fluorescent lights, and read Katie's journal. Nothing belongs to Katie, not any longer. Or, it is all mine: her detritus, her daily life, even her secrets. I don't have to share them with anyone.

I fly out to Boston that spring to attend the wedding of a friend from college. The whole weekend I feel alternately humored and suffocated. Perhaps I am selfish and do not want anyone else to fall in love. Or, I am intimidated and unsure of myself. Or, I want to warn everyone about how this marriage might end, however improbable. It is obvious to me that I have made a foolish decision to attend. I am not even in the wedding party or a part of the service.

My friend is Russian, and at the rehearsal dinner we drink too much vodka. I halfheartedly hit on a married bridesmaid, who details at great length the failures of her own marriage. Really, I am desperate to confide the secret of Katie's death, to practice its power, but my friend has warned everyone in advance about my situation. He has asked them to treat me gingerly, with a sense of deference. It is a sensitivity and kindness on his part, and it magnifies both my need and my shame. I am marked as someone special. I am sympathized with. I have no secret.

A few blocks from the restaurant, I throw up in the bushes in front of the Prudential building. I pass out on the T and wake up at the end of the line, last train, Braintree. I spend seventy-five dollars to take a cab back to the hotel. The next afternoon, before the wedding, I buy a new pair of very expensive shoes. I feel uncertain and unstable. I try to make small talk, but I can only think of one thing to talk about, the inevitable subject I am terrified to broach. I sit for the beginning of the reception, the first dance, the toasts, and when the music picks up, I leave early.

6.

We are standing in front of the People's Palace of Bucharest, considering Katie's job offer to live in Romania for the rest of the summer and the following year. It is late August and hot. This part of the city is quiet and empty. Katie asks me, again, if it is really what I want to do. Am I ready to leave Miami, to move again? Can we really make a life in Romania?

Each time she asks, we are exhausted and afraid. We feel a little older. We have talked out every detail, and now we look at each other. Katie is holding my hands and standing very close. Her eyes are bright, and she will not look down. I hate seeing her like this, as I know she hates, more than anything, feeling vulnerable.

Do we really want to do this? she asks again, and I know she means, *I know how much you love me, and I love you, and still, this might not work out. This might be a terrible, terrible mistake we are making. And once we make it, we will not be able to walk it back, not really, not without consequences.*

I cannot tell all of this story.

I can no longer distinguish conscience from will.

Katie does not speak to me from the grave. Her voice does not carry across the grasses of the nature preserve and whisper stories about our life together or challenge any part of what she says now. What I make her say. Even what is preserved in letters and journals and photographs is perfected in conversations with friends and family members, in an order I continue to assemble, which refuses any certain shape, which I will one day completely imagine; all of it diminishes daily.

For weeks before Katie's death date, and then again before her birthday, I am edgy and irritable. I stop doing things. I spend time alone, and I think only about her death, and I hope to grieve, however contrived, because if I grieve again I will feel better and surrender, for a while, the burden. I will the emotion. I complete the ritual.

I am not dead. I do not die symbolic deaths. I will not imagine some figurative transformation of death and say it has become truth and beauty. Death has no hypothetical aspect, however I have witnessed it. It is not mastered through ritual and practice.

But there is this. Under the lights of the neon billboards making shadows across the empty palace, I pause a moment. I sit down on the bench and look up at Katie. I cannot change my answer, but I know the sound of my voice there, and I speak with certainty; again and again, I begin the sequence. I must. It is my obligation. We will leave together. *Yes.*

Alone to Tell Thee

Had I really once believed I could lose no part of Katie?

If you had asked me before we left for Romania what Katie and I meant to do there, I would have said we were continuing a life. We were going to work. We were eager to travel. I would have defended the marriage as loving and honest, and however I might have articulated its limits, I would feel no melancholy for them.

Katie would not have tried so hard to explain things. She would have said that if some pattern or habit made a provision for our life together, then we lived that life. However well we liked it, we loved each other. Then, as now, I did not know every part of Katie's life that continued into our relationship or preceded it, but I knew the parts that began with it. Wasn't it what Katie had asked of the marriage: to take her to new places, to do new things? This was the Katie I knew and loved: my wife. For all of us it was this Katie—wanderer or truant, prophet or prodigal—who had died on the mountain.

I had a story to tell about this world and how it seemed to compulsively make sense; that it incentivized risk and accommodated broad intrusions until it decided to not be passive; that its response became overwhelming, complete, and final. Irrational and, very suddenly, deadly. I wondered what I had bartered with the universe in order to gain this sense of exception, whether it followed me now; shouldn't the raw statistical improbability of it make everyone I know exempt to future tragedy?

How closely I had come to violating it that night on the ridge, as the bear moved completely afield of me, making its wide sweep toward the stream. Even when I doubled back across the bear's path, it was indifferent to me. It pawed at Katie, with increasing violence and focus, and ignored me. So, I watched. In this way I was made a witness. That I did not, and might never, understand what I witnessed seemed beside the point. I had been there. I could describe it.

In the minor anecdotes of her life, Katie does not die again. Each time I imagine her death, I remember more of myself and think less of her. Willing or unwilling, there is always present the possibility of intervention. It teases the promise of a life different from this one, a continuing life I'm not sure I still want.

After his ordeal Job receives a piece of money and one gold earring from each person he has ever known. He is a survivor, now. His voice is articulate. Each piece of jewelry is both ornament and currency. It is worn individually to express wealth or bartered for still another kind of wealth that accumulates in excess of what the Lord has compensated Job for his suffering. *The Lord blessed the latter part of Job's life more than the former.* His redemption is ordained. The restitution is, finally, secular. Job's new family both consoles and celebrates his return to the world of the living.

For the death anniversary, as before the funeral, I wrote a group email. I put together another simple ceremony. Again, our families met at the nature preserve, then walked to the clearing where we had spread Katie's ashes. We drank tea and orange juice in Katie's honor. We read prayers. Nieces turned handstands, as Katie had taught them, while Ben sang "Let the Mystery Be." I had imagined it would be a moment of comfort and communion, maybe even reconciliation, but it felt instead like a performance. Rather than her death, the ritual acknowledged a year of grief. Much as we might fear and imagine it, Katie would not die again.

We were two groups now, wary of each other's comfort—Wife and Sister, Widower and Family, Performers and Watchers—and staking competing claims. Even Katie's death site seemed prospected. Katie's father made a sign we posted near the entrance, while Judy made another sign to take into the preserve, while I made a speech. Who was listening, who had not also been there a year earlier? What could I say now that wouldn't move the emphasis away from Katie's death and instead seek consolation before or after it? The service comforted me, but Katie's family seemed tired of the traveling show. I assured myself as I had on the mountain the night of her death—*there is nothing I can do about this*—and again I resented feeling so resigned in the moment to loss.

Was this the duty of the survivor, to narrow the loss to some manageable part, transform it, and then move forward? Katie was a saint and a martyr, a point of comparison, a transformative figure, a symbol. An occasion to remember her death and a reminder of her absence in the world. She was no longer Katie. For me the death date was also a powerful reminder of watching Katie die, but I could not say that in the nature preserve. It seemed too self-focused.

I stayed the week at my brother's home in Chicago. Ed and his family drove me to the city, on their way back to Indiana. I would follow by bus in a few days. I said that the worst was over, that, in the end, I had again survived the day. My family congratulated me and said the next year would be easier; the second year, which now began.

Did I understand the obligations of the widower: that it was better to gather Katie's family together, however reluctantly, than to let them be? To plan a day of activities no one seemed especially eager to undertake, because it would be worse to do nothing? That afternoon I felt insincere and only partially there. Perhaps the death anniversary was a command performance. I wanted Katie's family to see that I missed her. I tried to display a range of emotions that was no longer present in my everyday life. What had happened to those emotions? I missed them.

Grief had pitch and scale now; the key was familiar. If I was hypervigilant of what were called "triggers"—loud noises, too little sleep, large animals—then I also understood the limits of vigilance. I would not wait to be overwhelmed. I hedged. I became better at anticipating when I might grieve for Katie. Here was something I learned, which no one had told me before Katie's death: it felt good to physically grieve. I initiated different, less intense sequences. Nostalgia and remorse. Guilt and inadequacy. The effect was to feel less often hysterical and more present in my continuing life.

I could no longer explain my life with Katie without also analyzing it. Yet, each successive argument changed my conclusions. Katie was beautiful and heroic. Her death was tragic but inspiring. Her memory was everyone's so that it would never be lost. Which one was right? If they were all right, where was I supposed to keep the emphasis? The sentiments seemed true enough, and yet none was especially real or felt. Where was the consolation of Katie's life, except that it should be a beautiful thing to remember together and become more so with time? And if I still felt angry with Katie for dying, if I expressed anger at the circumstances, there would always come the rejoinder: *I just don't see it,* a friend would say. *I mean, I always thought you guys seemed really happy together.*

That spring I hid pictures of Katie in various objects. I went to the copy shop and had business cards printed on cream-colored stock. On one side: the photo of Katie I kept on my desk. On the other: a poem I had written for her that she had liked. I put a card in my wallet, between my driver's license and credit card. I put another card in the glove compartment of my car. One was stuck deep in a computer bag, so that it might fall out whenever I took my laptop to the coffee shop or across campus. The idea was to surprise myself where I might not otherwise see her and also to jostle some new sequence of memories whose practice might, with time, become a habit.

Katie's death presaged all varieties of calamity that never bore out. The small tragedy of a missed call, a late arrival, or a nasty fall did not escalate into broken bones, abductions, and car wrecks. I would clutch and wait: nothing. The inhabited world seemed again overly safe and insulated. I feared being so protected. I loved it.

I expected rational thought to be purposeful after Katie's death. I suppose it was, though not in the manner I had hoped. Where I wanted to arrive at nuanced and sensitive conclusions, I became instead exceedingly skilled at rationalization and avoidance. Where I expected a certain foreboding in nature, I faced nothing and waited for time to pass. Nature was not changed. I marked off days that became weeks, then months, then a year. At the end of that year, I gathered everyone together for a memorial service, and in many ways it felt like variations on a theme. One year of living after Katie's death was over, and while we would never live that year again, there would be successive years.

The memorial card in my wallet curled at its edges. I replaced it with another card. I checked that the other cards were in their right places, and I waited to be surprised. I made more cards and mailed them to Katie's family. Perhaps I was the connection to a part of

Katie's life they tolerated but had never really understood: global health volunteer, graduate student, expatriate. Their hometown girl, choosing to leave home. My Katie looked back from the fun-house mirror: recognizable but distorted, at odd angles to the truth. Here was a mirror they could carry in their wallets.

Hadn't it been, in many ways, my year of consolations? Of making the story of Katie's life and death, and our marriage, something fixed and remote, so that I could stand at a distance from it? I wanted to see us clearly, and I also wanted to live after us, in the shadow any shortcomings might make on my continuing life. Didn't that shadow make it easier to recognize the worst of myself in our history and so step away from it entirely?

More and more, it seemed I would not be held accountable for such distinctions. Instead, they gave a certain glamour to sitting alone in my room next to the garage. They began new arguments no one else wanted to continue. Katie was fixed individually in our memories, and I was impatient with the witness.

After our walk through the preserve, Judy had everyone over to her house for a potluck barbeque. Family, then friends, then neighbors filled the back porch with casseroles, bowls of chips, fruit-and-vegetable plates, deviled eggs. We sat for a while, making small talk about the election primaries, teaching, plans for travel. We took turns saying nice things about Katie, speaking in generalities so that we might all participate in the acknowledgment and affection.

I said that Katie and I had always liked to visit her mother's house. I described in detail how the first thing we did each time was unpack, say hello, and go for a run. What I wanted to say was that I imagined the world that allowed Katie to die quickly might also be a merciful one. I wanted to insist that a world absent of Katie was a world in which our lives had to have more value, in which we needed to do more to honor Katie, to try harder, to make the most of what little time we had left. Instead, I rattled off a different and equally meaningless yet more personally felt consolation. Everyone agreed with its sentiment. For a moment we all seemed to agree we would feel good together. Consolations were at least something to fill the intervening silences.

In Bangladesh Katie and I survived monsoons, typhoons, and flooding in our small cement rooms that lost electricity and filled with water. In Miami we legged out hurricanes, reading *Harry Potter* by flashlight and cooking cans of beans on the outdoor grill. In Romania a blizzard, then an earthquake.

Were these new silences between Katie's family and me a sign of restitution? Were they meaningful? Did they protect the memory or poison it? We had around us our communities. Every polite conversation and moment of small talk contained the secret of Katie's death. Sometimes we did not name it. I had been there. Most times, I didn't acknowledge it. Katie's family and I measured each other for the awareness of a distinction and kept our distances. However we grieved, Katie's death was the point toward and from which our lives gathered, as prelude and memory. Together, and individually, we only lived after it.

Was there one more thing I knew, which I might tell, or to which I might confess, that would make continue these moments of disclosure; and, if I did choose to disclose them, would the telling itself be still one last rite of grief, a part of it kept back so as to lose neither the feeling nor the end the ritual? Had I secreted that knowledge away, and would its arrival one day surprise me?

I wanted there to be a secret. I wanted to pursue its origins in the cities where we had lived and visited, in the songs and stories Katie had loved, in the movies that would seem one day full of outdated slang and bulldozed skylines—fashions that suggest, all at once, a different time and place, but also a changed moment, an idiom, a place that can only be imagined with such certainty that the place never really existed. I needed to believe there was something more that might explain everything more clearly, and yet, the fact of Katie's death made me certain I had all of the pieces in front of me. I could not explain the absence of sense in Katie's pain, suffering, and death because I did not see any.

If I tell the story of Katie's death, years later, will it still be a confession?

Both the death and the marriage are lost to consolation, witness, and revelation: the arbitrary survivals perpetuated in myth. I have only Job's silence during and after his test. His surrender to the will of God is also the absence of a protest, the evidence of a faith, all evidence to the contrary, in divine order and mercy.

For Katie's death, and my witness of it, I was comforted, loved, and made a part of a new family. That community sympathized with me during the year I lived in Indiana. So, perhaps my restitution to the family was ordered, immediate, and complete. My lamentation of Katie's absence exists within an ordered universe. In this version of the story, I am Job, the messenger is the bear, and both Katie's family and my family comfort me.

Alternately, I might be the community that comforts Job by receiving a story about death and unreason from the natural world. Katie is the messenger. It is unclear to whom, and with whom, I offer restitution and also to whom I tell this story. To what extent that restitution happens is made a test of faith for someone else. I do not yet know Job, but I ready my offering to him.

Or, I am Job's messenger. I escaped Katie's death in order to relay its fact and witness to Katie's family, my family, and everyone who grieved for her absence in the world. Everyone is Job. Everyone's faith is tested. Because I am only Job's messenger, my fate is unclear. No one comforts me. I am not meant to lament or to be consoled and instructed.

I might one day become that best part of Katie continuing in the world: wise, centered, empathic. Perhaps I will omit the story of the death from the witness of the trauma, in order to clarify a sense of the continuing life. The term here, I think, is still *consolation*: to perform the lie that insists meaning, duration, and stability into our very brief lives. The terms of that witness are immoral, unjust, and absolute. I fear both accepting and being judged by them. They make the events of a life arbitrary and Katie's death meaningless.

In Bucharest, at night, I sometimes knocked on the wooden bedframe as I fell asleep. It was a superstition I had learned from a colleague in Chicago who was fond of mythology. I knocked the wood so that the spirit world would not hear me confessing my worst fears, which, according to the legend, I was required to say out loud, lest they become true. I found it comforting to do this every night until it became a ritual and then a habit, a pattern I could not disrupt without imagining greater consequences for the interruption. Sometimes, I woke in the middle of the night so as not to miss the ritual. When I felt especially vulnerable, I said a short prayer. I rolled over in the bed and clung to Katie, who woke enough to pull my arm across her chest. And then, I fell asleep.

Winners of the River Teeth Literary Nonfiction Prize

Five Shades of Shadow
Tracy Daugherty

The Untouched Minutes
Donald Morrill

Where the Trail Grows Faint:
A Year in the Life of a
Therapy Dog Team
Lynne Hugo

The World Before Mirrors
Joan Connor

House of Good Hope:
A Promise for a Broken City
Michael Downs

The Enders Hotel: A Memoir
Brandon R. Schrand

An Inside Passage
Kurt Caswell

Test Ride on the Sunnyland Bus:
A Daughter's Civil Rights Journey
Ana Maria Spagna

A Double Life:
Discovering Motherhood
Lisa Catherine Harper

Mountains of Light: Seasons
of Reflection in Yosemite
R. Mark Liebenow

So Far, So Good
Ralph Salisbury

Young Widower: A Memoir
John W. Evans

To order or obtain more information on these or other University
of Nebraska Press titles, visit nebraskapress.unl.edu.

CPSIA information can be obtained at www.ICGtesting.com
Printed in the USA
BVOW07s0144060214

344088BV00001B/1/P